SIX STEPS TO
CUSTOMER HAPPINESS

SIX STEPS TO CUSTOMER HAPPINESS

MARK PRICE

www.engaging.works

STOUR
PUBLISHING

An imprint of
David Fickling Books

Published in Great Britain in 2019 by Stour Publishing
an imprint of David Fickling Books

31 Beaumont Street,
Oxford,
OX1 2NP

www.davidficklingbooks.com

British Library Cataloguing-in-Publication Data
A catalogue record for this book is available on
request from the British Library

ISBN 978 1 78845 165 9

Typeset in 11/17 pt Minion Pro by
Falcon Oast Graphic Art Ltd, www.falcon.uk.com

Printed and bound in Great Britain by Clays Ltd, Elcograf S.p.A.

Contents

INTRODUCTION

One of my favourite stories about how to deal with customers hails from South Africa. It concerns Raymond Ackerman, the man who built a four-store, Cape Town-based chain called Pick n Pay into one of Africa's largest retailers, with more than 124 supermarkets, 14 hypermarkets and 179 franchised outlets. I know his son, Gareth, quite well, and on one of my visits to Cape Town, he told me a somewhat surprising tale about his dad.

Apparently, Raymond Ackerman deliberately fixed the water jets on his car so they spurted water either side of the vehicle, rather than onto the windscreen. Whenever he stopped at traffic lights and saw someone walking past carrying a bag of shopping with the branding of a competitor, he'd flick the switch sending a spurt of water in the direction of the unassuming shopper.

As the no doubt very cross pedestrian looked

incredulously at the source of this intrusion into their otherwise pleasant day, Raymond would leap out of his car, feigning a look of horror and remorse.

'I am so so sorry,' he would say. 'I have no idea how that happened. I was just trying to clear the dust from my windscreen and then . . .'

If the supermarket boss was lucky, the mildly soaked pedestrian might soften a little, whereupon Raymond would leap in with an intriguing offer.

'Please, let me make this up to you,' he'd say. 'Do you have far to go? Let me give you a lift.'

According to the family legend, once the shopper got into the car, Raymond Ackerman saw it as his challenge to convert them to Pick n Pay by the time he reached their front doorstep. His patter was that Pick n Pay was a vastly superior store to the one his passenger currently shopped in. With determination like this, I have no doubt the ploy was constantly successful and he won another Pick n Pay customer each time.

Like I say, I love this story. However, while you cannot help but admire the tenacity of this win-one-customer-at-a-time approach, and it undoubtedly shows fantastic dedication to the cause, I am bound to say this is not a customer strategy I would necessarily favour or recommend. My philosophy has always centred on valuing the customers you already have, rather than constantly looking around to bring in new ones. To me, it is just more effective, and I am not sure many businesses can afford to spend so much time building up their customer base on such a labour-intensive basis either.

The reason I have turned my attention to the customer, after my previous book, *Fairness for All*, looked at the miracles that can be performed once a business has fully engaged its workforce, is because I passionately believe there is a real need to transform the way we deal with customers today. While customer service is much talked about, I think far too many businesses are missing out here or spending a fortune on customer service strategies that are wide of the mark.

Too much is made of the importance of bringing in a steady flow of new faces to sustain the bottom line, or highlighting ways to maximise a person's spend once they visit your business, or increasing margins without losing customer loyalty. While everyone has a role, what no one ever seems to talk about is the simple art of making a customer happy.

In *Fairness for All* I discussed my belief that the supreme purpose of a CEO is to maximise the happiness of their team. This translates into employees giving more, which guarantees customers get more. A win–win situation. (It also means that suppliers, communities and shareholders benefit too.) In this book, I would like to extend this core strategy to include the absolute necessity of focusing on the happiness of customers. I want to show you how to deliver customer happiness and create a standard of service and delivery in your organisation that will consistently put smiles on the faces of your customers, day in and day out.

This goal is more important today than it has ever been. There is barely a business out there that has not been touched by the digital revolution. Whatever it is you sell, the chances are there are dozens of online outlets that can deliver it to your customers faster and more cheaply. Retailers need to give people a good reason to choose them.

Gone are the days when companies should focus on 'acquiring' customers or 'converting' them. (At least I hope they are.) When did you last hear anyone tell you they were delighted to be 'acquired' by a brand? Who wants to be 'converted'? I know I don't. Now, more than ever, people value personalised service, delivered promptly and hopefully with some sort of experience attached.

This is what makes customers happy.

Getting customer service right has become the most powerful differentiator for brands, and the only way to do this right is to ensure happy customers. It is about creating true empathy and connection, every single time you connect. Screw-up just one single aspect of your offering and it'll be out there, posted on social media in perpetuity. A hard-earned brand reputation can be damaged in a single tweet.

For many businesses this will mean a completely different way of thinking.

Step One

Love the Customers You Have

Key points

- Acquiring new customers is between 5 and 25 times *more expensive* than simply looking after the ones you have.
- Word of mouth recommendation is a more powerful way to connect with customers than any advert.

I was about seven years old when I got my first insight into the power of just what can happen when you make a customer happy. One of the two small businesses that my father started and ran was a grocery wholesale operation, delivering goods all over the county. As a kid, I would go along to help him before and after school and in the school holidays. They were long days, and hard work lugging boxes about, but I enjoyed spending time with him and listening to his stories.

One day, we were on the way home when we passed a small shop. Peering through the large picture windows as we went by, we saw ladders, tins of paint and boxes strewn across the dust-sheet-covered floor, and shelves in the process of being put up.

'I wonder what they're going to be selling in there,' said my father, pulling over and yanking up the handbrake of the van with a loud metallic creak.

Inwardly, I sighed. I knew my dad wouldn't be put off going off to investigate so it wasn't worth asking, even though it was late in the day and I clearly wanted to go home for my tea.

We went in. 'I see you are opening up a shop,' said my father with a friendly smile. 'I hope you don't mind me asking, but what are you going to sell?'

The other man returned my dad's smile and put out his hand to shake my father's.

'It's going to be a grocery shop,' he replied.

The response elicited an even broader smile from my father.

'Perfect! I sell confectionery, sweets, biscuits, all sorts and would be very happy to supply you,' he said.

The shopkeeper paused, looking unsure as to how to react. I thought he even looked a little embarrassed.

'Listen, that's a really kind offer, but the thing is, we're opening in a few days. To be honest with you, money is a bit tight. I've spent most of what I had on all this.' He gestured towards the jumble of DIY equipment and the almost completed shelving units behind him.

My dad nodded thoughtfully.

'Look, don't worry about that,' he said. 'I'll give you some cases of biscuits and I'll come back when you've sold them. You can pay me then.'

I couldn't help but admire my dad's approach. Even then I could see it was a fantastically smart way to get a new customer. Sadly though, the shopkeeper still looked doubtful.

'I don't want to sound rude, because it is a really kind offer, but I am nervous about the risk of taking on a whole box wholesale.'

'Not to worry, you can take half a box,' my father shot straight back, without hesitation.

The shopkeeper looked genuinely grateful and they shook hands on the deal. My father and I hurried back to the car, opened a number of boxes of biscuits and split them in two. We carried the packets of biscuits back to the shop and arranged them on the shelf.

The two men chatted a little further and then we were on our way. It was late afternoon by then and my stomach was rumbling irritably. I knew full well that even when we arrived home there was still the lengthy process of unloading the van and itemising the day's work to go through.

It was almost dark by the time we arrived home. Without saying anything, I walked to the back of the van, climbed in and started to move the boxes. Meanwhile, dad ripped the top off a cardboard box and used it as a note pad to start totting everything up.

About ten minutes in, I heard dad tut with annoyance.

'Mark, I've made a terrible mistake,' he exclaimed, turning to face me. 'There were 24 packets in this box and I've only given that man 11. There are 13 left here.'

I stood in silence as my father weighed up what to do. I already knew – and dreaded – the solution.

'We need to go back,' he declared.

'Dad, it's so late and we've been out all day,' I said weakly, knowing I was speaking in vain.

'Nope, we've got to go back,' he repeated emphatically.

That's exactly what we did. We climbed back in the van and drove the 20-miles plus back to the unopened shop. The shopkeeper was, quite naturally, overwhelmed by my father's honesty and the fact he had gone out of his way to drive all that way to correct his mistake. Not only that, Dad also said that since it was his mistake, the shopkeeper didn't have to repay him for the 12th packet.

This was, of course, an extraordinary demonstration of above-and-beyond customer service. However, it is the footnote to this story that shows how powerful it can be to make your customers happy.

That shopkeeper went on to be enormously successful and opened a chain of shops. Each time he opened a new store, my father was one of the first suppliers he'd call and he only ever dealt with him for those products. One day, the chain got to such a size that it began to make sense to deal directly with either the producer or with one of the really big wholesale suppliers, rather than using my father as an intermediary. The shopkeeper wouldn't hear of it.

'I'll stick with you,' he told my father. 'You looked after me when I started.'

It was a huge lesson: make your customers happy and keep them happy, and you'll have a customer for life.

I often think of this story when I look at the marketing efforts of businesses. So often it is geared to acquiring new customers, while virtually ignoring the ones they have. Yet, depending on which study you believe, acquiring new customers is between 5 and 25 times *more expensive* than simply looking after the ones you have.

Certain sectors are worse than others. Banks, utility companies and retailers are serial offenders in this respect. They spend hundreds of thousands of their advertising budgets shouting about fantastic introductory offers or price cuts to attract new people through the door. I often imagine the reaction of bemused loyal customers, who must be wondering why they are being so roundly ignored. And not to mention the frustration or annoyance at annual renewal time when the threat of leaving elicits a better price. Why waste time and resources on seeking out a new customer when all you need to do is keep the ones you have happy?

If you are not convinced, or need cold hard financial

facts to persuade you, consider this: increasing customer retention rates by just 5 per cent, in other words keeping them happy so they don't walk out of the door, increases profits by between 25 to 95 per cent.[1] Also, while we are on financial reasons to think about customer happiness, it's worth pointing out that investors and analysts use 'churn rate', which is the percentage of customers that abandon a company in a given period, as a metric to evaluate the underlying health of a firm. The more people that leave, the more shaky its outlook. The markets want you to keep your existing customers happy.

I suspect that the reason so many businesses focus on customer acquisition, rather than keeping the ones they have, is because they accept it as a given that customers will move on. The thought process probably goes along the lines of: we need a steady number of new faces to replace the ones who get fed up and go. It's a reasonable proposition as far as it goes, but the pendulum has swung too far. Thinking in this way becomes a self-fulfilling prophecy. By virtually ignoring your current customer

[1] Frederick Reichheld, Bain & Company, *Prescription for cutting costs*, 2003.

base, you are practically driving them away. Not to mention the fact that if you are constantly topping-up your customer numbers with the promise of low low prices (*get one now, no competitor can beat us!*) then you'll only attract deal seekers, who will move on at the first sniff of a better deal elsewhere.

Looking at customer numbers in the context of churn, where a business knows it will lose, say 20,000 customers a year and therefore needs to find 20,000 to replace them, makes the task mechanistic and devoid of humanity. No one has a reason to ask: why are 20,000 people a year walking away? What have we done to make them unhappy? Is there something we can do to turn that around? It's only when you start to look behind the bald facts and statistics that you really understand what a problem is. And we do need to know how our customers feel and if they are unhappy.

None of this is to say businesses should not seek new customers. Of course they need to do that. It is just that the emphasis is all wrong. Try and find out what your marketing department spends on recruiting new customers as opposed to retaining current ones. Our main focus should be on keeping our existing customers happy so they stay for longer.

And here's the thing that is most often missed. Loyal, happy customers are the best marketing you can have. People are more likely to respond positively to a friend or relative's recommendation, or even a stranger's for that matter, than to an advert. Nielsen's 2015 Global Trust in Advertising report repeated findings from previous years – people don't trust advertising, at least not as much as they trust recommendations from friends and consumer opinions expressed online. According to the report, which surveyed more than 28,000 internet respondents in 56 countries, 92 per cent of consumers say they trust recommendations from friends and family above all other forms of advertising – an increase of 18 per cent since 2007. Online consumer reviews rank as the second most trusted source, with 70 per cent of global consumers surveyed online indicating they trust messages on this platform – an increase of 15 per cent in four years.

When I joined the John Lewis Partnership in the early 1980s, the company's constitution stated that money should not be spent on advertising, rather that it should be spent on resolving customer issues, no matter how unreasonable and unjust they might seem. I believe at that time around 2 per cent of turnover was spent on 'Goodwill' to keep existing customers loyal and happy. John Lewis has been repaid many times over, and is consistently ranked not only Britain's favourite retailer, but also Britain's favourite brand. But we'll return to the theme of marketing later.

Give Great Service – Always

Whenever I speak about retail at conferences around the world, the same question always comes up: but what about Amazon? How can anyone selling anything compete in a digital age? We have to keep finding new customers.

I have to concede that, yes, very many customers are indeed happy with Amazon. Million upon million, in fact. What's not to like about being able to shop anywhere, anytime, at the touch of a button and have your goods delivered to your doorstep? This does not, however, mean that Amazon has the monopoly on happy customers. Far from it, in fact.

The debate here should be about what service people want and what aspects they value the most. Believe it or not, there is room for more than just one player.

Happy customers vote with their feet. It is the reason why, when the destruction of bookshops was predicted at the hands of the mighty Amazon, many are thriving today. Take Waterstones as an example. While the chain did seriously stumble under the onslaught of Amazon for a while, and came close to filing for bankruptcy, it has become a success story under the guidance of James Daunt who joined in May 2011. Instead of slashing book prices in an unedifying (and unwinnable) race to the bottom, Daunt focused on what the customer really wanted out of the book-buying experience. He increased the number of books available in Waterstones stores by about a quarter and empowered his booksellers to choose the range of books they stocked in their individual shops. Daunt figured that individual store managers knew much more about what people liked in their local area, and he was completely right. The chain hasn't just survived Amazon: it has grown. It is opening new stores, is in profit, and in April 2018, after activist hedge fund Elliott Advisors bought a controlling stake, there was talk of returning it to the stock market.

The Waterstones story reminds me of an interesting debate I had many years ago while still at the John Lewis Partnership, prior to joining Waitrose. I was speaking to Stuart Rose (now Lord Rose) and he had some very firm views on pleasing customers.

'It's about the right product, at the right price, in the right place,' he declared emphatically. 'All efficiently served to the customer.'

While I saw his point, I argued quite strongly at the time that these were the fundamentals of retailing, but the icing is the *experience* the customer has when they make their purchase. Yes, all those other factors were crucial, but my focus would always be on making sure we offered the exact right environment and level of personal service to put a smile on their face. This is the thing the customer remembers the most.

Going back to the perennial Amazon question, the internet giant scores very highly on Stuart Rose's metric of the right product, at the right price, in the right place. These are all things Amazon does incredibly well. You can navigate their website easily, quickly find the product you want out of a selection of millions of items, and be fairly sure it is being sold at a very keen price. Once you've paid for your basket of goods, you can be equally confident that what you have ordered will turn up when they said it would. It's a brilliantly executed service, there is no doubt about that.

Now, ask yourself this. Have you built a bond with Amazon? If something goes wrong and the product is faulty, or gets delivered elsewhere by mistake, or isn't quite what you expected, are you confident they'll rectify the issue immediately? Or do you inwardly sigh because you know you'll most likely spend hours trying to find a real person to speak to to sort out the problem? There are millions of satisfied Amazon customers out there, but there are some who are concerned that complaining to the business or returning goods is not as straightforward as it should be.

This is not to knock Amazon at all. Hats off to an enormously successful business model. It is an aggressive, efficient and hugely convenient service. However, you have to ask what will happen to the retail operation in five, ten or 20 years time. By this time, their competitive advantage of scale growth will have plateaued. It's hugely likely that many other digital services will have entered the market with a similar offering, but move things forward with a *far more personal service level*. That's when it will get really interesting.

Businesses don't need to wait for this to happen, though. Every firm with something to sell should be thinking about personal and personalised service now, online or off. Just take a look at tails.com a personalised dog food service for your pooch. Instead of being product first, as most retail businesses are, its focus is on what is right for your dog. What is it, over and above product, price and environment, that will make their customers happy? Yes, today's market is more competitive than ever, thanks in great part to digital, but there is still a way to stand out.

———————— **Create a Connection** ————————

Firstly, a confession. When I joined Waitrose in 1998 as its first-ever marketing director, one of my first acts was to change the John Lewis Partnership constitution to allow us to advertise. The governing principles of the organisation then forbade any sort of promotion, instead favouring 'Goodwill' spending, as I explained earlier.

Hold on a moment, you may be thinking, *only a few pages earlier, you said firms should love the customers they have, not chase around looking for fresh ones.* And you'd be right. The reason for the change was because we were being hit very hard by aggressive competition from the likes of Tesco, which had pulled out all the stops to overtake Sainsbury's to become the market leader. In all the noise among the biggest players, it was beginning to feel like Waitrose had been somewhat shouted down. However, while the way was opened up for Waitrose to advertise for the first time, I was more focused than ever on my core belief of loving my existing customers above and beyond all other considerations.

To make customers happy, you need to create a connection. Even before we lined up our first national newspaper adverts, I'd thought long and hard about how we'd forge that connection. So when we first advertised it was aimed at our existing customers. The adverts were designed to help them understand Waitrose's ethical stance and quality commitment, and thus the price differential and value in Waitrose. They could then better explain to their friends and family why they shopped at Waitrose and become apostles for the brand. We advertised in the magazines, papers and TV programmes that our customers read or watched. It wasn't a campaign to persuade people to shop in Waitrose, but rather to help Waitrose spread the word through its customers.

Later on, I expanded on the idea and introduced a scheme where customers who signed up to our loyalty card were given a free cup of tea or coffee. If they spent £5 on a weekday, they were given a free newspaper too.

It struck me that this would be the perfect way to give customers a treat in-store. Who wouldn't enjoy a few moments relaxing with a hot drink and a newspaper after a weekly shop? Obviously, our customers enjoyed it very much too. In a short period of time, Waitrose became the second largest provider of coffee in the UK, pouring our grateful customers more than one million brews a week.

Of course, the one thing everyone is guaranteed to love is a pleasant surprise. Thus, we encouraged those working in the shops to carry out regular 'random acts of kindness'. One Father's Day we handed out free Toblerones to all the dads who came in-store. If a colleague overheard someone say it was their birthday or they had just passed an exam, they would be given a small gift. Ideas like this consume a tiny fraction of the marketing budget, but their positive effect is exponential.

When your ambition is to look after the customers you already have, it opens up a host of opportunities. Of course, it's very helpful if you know all about them, how much they spend with you and how often. In times gone by this was discovered through personal relationships, whereas now the focus is more on mining data, which to me still feel very impersonal. But once you know about your customers, you'll understand any needs you are not currently servicing. In the supermarket context, this all relates to the somewhat unlovable term 'share of stomach'. Basically, it means how much of your weekly food intake is catered for by the grocery store and how much is looked after elsewhere through trips to restaurants or takeaways. The shopkeeper's aim is to get more of a share of a customer's stomach, and this means encouraging people to shop more frequently and to spend more when they do. This is exactly what Waitrose did with its tea, coffee and newspapers. The free drinks were about making customers come in more often. The £5 minimum spend for a newspaper was geared towards getting them to spend more.

I don't think any of our customers felt they were being marketed to. Quite the opposite. The little extras made them feel loved and cherished.

The strategy also brought in new customers. By creating this strong connection, our happy customers told their friends, who tried it for themselves and told their friends. If you as a business are obsessed by churn and replacing lost customers, remember this: word of mouth recommendation is a more powerful way to connect with customers than any advert. Even in the digital world, we all still vastly prefer the word of our friends to random marketing messages from people or places we have no connection with. It's the reason why online sellers focus so much on the power of personal recommendations: *you/ your peer group liked this product, so you'll love X*. It's so much more powerful than screaming from the roof tops that if you shop with ABC Co, you'll get 20 per cent off.

That's not connecting with people on a personal level: it's telling the world.

Yes, the adverts I argued for at Waitrose were effective, and I have no regrets about pushing the organisation in this way. However, I still believe our best work was done in showing our appreciation and loyalty to the customers we already had. By far.

LOVE THE CUSTOMER YOU HAVE – WINNERS

Zappos

Most call centres use something known as 'average handle time', or the equivalent, to gauge their efficiency. The (not very subtle) unsaid subtext is: the quicker you can get through it and onto the next one, the better. US shoe and fashion retailer Zappos thinks the opposite way. The firm's philosophy is, if they have a customer's undivided attention for even five minutes, then it is the equivalent of a five-minute-long Zappos infomercial, delivered right into their customer's home.

Top of Zappos' long list of refreshing company values is to put the customer first. There are no set policies on how to do this, and staff on the front line are empowered to do whatever they feel is the right thing for the customer as an individual. Bureaucracy is kept to a minimum; there are no standard scripts and there is definitely no place for 'average handle time'. Which is how one of its customer service reps was able to spend an astonishing 10 hours and 29 minutes on the phone to a customer. How is that for loving the customer you have?

Zappos was founded in 1999 with the idea that it would be 'insane' and 'fanatical' in the way it treated customers. Central to the strategy was a call centre in Las Vegas where 500 people work, each of whom has received seven weeks training in how to make a customer happy. The stories of how they've managed to do this are legendary in the company, which celebrates each one – because when customers are happy they talk about it, they tweet and they blog. One rep sent flowers to a woman who had ordered six different pairs of shoes because her feet were damaged by a medical treatment. On another occasion, a customer services rep physically went to a rival shoe store to get a specific pair of shoes to a woman staying at the Mandalay Hotel, Las Vegas, because Zappos were out of stock. Another time, a free pair of shoes was sent out overnight to a best man who had forgotten his when he packed for the wedding he was playing a key role in.

Zappos was snapped up by Amazon in 2009 for $1.2 billion, but the CEO, Tony Hsieh, has worked hard to keep the firm's extraordinary customer first culture. The strategy is simple: make the customer happy, no matter what.

Interestingly, if you go onto Zappos.com, you will see that there is nothing particularly incredible about their prices. There is little advertising and no coupons or discounts. Yet, the Zappos customer is incredibly loyal. They certainly are not swayed by coupons and discounts from competitors, which is the normal staple promotion in the competitive world of clothing and footwear. In fact, 75 per cent of Zappos' purchases are from returning customers. These customers are comfortable in the fact that Zappos will always offer great customer service. This assurance is either through personal experience or via recommendations from friends. In fact, an impressive 44 per cent of Zappos customers heard about the brand via word of mouth.

Each of Zappos' policies is thought through from a

customer's point of view. Thus, the online retailer offers free returns, with no questions asked. In fact, they actively encourage customers to order multiple sizes if they are not sure, then they can return the ones that are not suitable. In the company's view, it is better to invest in existing customers than to offer multiple discounts and vouchers to entice in new ones.

Every potential Zappos employee is screened with their view on customer services in mind, as well as their technical capability to do the actual job. If they are not passionate about customers, they don't get in. Anyone who does get a job there is put through the same customer services training as those in the call centre, regardless of the position they eventually take up. Customer service really is a company-wide focus. The training comes in handy too, because all employees, right to the very top, handle customer service calls for at least ten hours a year.

There is even a programme where colleagues can recognise one another for providing great customer service. The co-worker bonus encourages every employee to nominate a colleague for a $50 payment for going above and beyond.

Being focused on customer service requires dedication and needs to be continually rewarded, celebrated and reinforced. Even after all the training and experience, everyone at the firm is constantly reminded of the one important rule: always do what is right for the customer.

LOVE THE CUSTOMERS YOU HAVE – LOSERS

Borders

If the Waterstones revival proved anything, it is that book buyers have a very special relationship with book lovers. Contrast the Waterstones experience with that of US-chain Borders. The chain was founded in 1971 by two young University of Michigan graduates, brothers Louis and Tom Borders. The pair loved books and came up with a system for tracking sales and inventory that could predict the pattern of demand in specific communities. After failing to interest any existing booksellers in their idea, they decided to go off and do it themselves.

Tailoring the stock to the likes and dislikes of the local communities it served was just the beginning of this book-store revolution. The brothers staffed their stores with employees who also loved the printed page. They prided themselves on their knowledge of the sections they were assigned to and willingly shared it with customers. The Borders stores themselves occupied areas with an unusually high square footage, but were carefully laid out with 'corridors' of high bookshelves, so customers could almost lose themselves in the library-like setting. People talked about Borders in hushed tones, as though it was one of the most pleasurable leisure time experiences they could have.

In 1992, discount department store chain Kmart bought Borders. Kmart already owned mall-based book chain Waldenbooks, but it had long struggled. No doubt they were very hopeful that some of the magic of Borders would rub off on Kmart. That wasn't to be.

Many of Borders' most experienced managers left the company, apparently uninterested in reviving the ailing Kmart book chain. They were, after all, book people and not keen to sell discounted clothes, jewellery and toys as well as paperbacks.

Three years later, Kmart spun off Borders and Waldenbooks via a flotation to the public. Inexplicably, this heralded an aggressive expansion of the retail footprint, including opening a large chain in the UK. This was foolish for a number of reasons. Firstly, because it was at a time when the book business was hurtling into the epicentre of the internet boom since Amazon had just launched as an online book-store. Secondly, the strategy involved Borders saddling itself with numerous lengthy and very expensive leases for physical stores, right at a time when customers started to wonder where all the magic had gone.

With no magical customer experience to draw them in, book buyers voted with their feet and gave the internet 'upstart' Amazon a try. To compound the misery, Borders tried to kick back by moving into CDs and DVDs, just as consumers were moving into digital delivery systems. It did, eventually, develop an e-reader, the Kobo, but only three years after Amazon came out with its Kindle.

Borders even fluffed its entrance to selling online, famously outsourcing its internet operation to Amazon, of all companies. It was essentially handing customers over to a bigger, better site in the formative years of e-commerce.

It would be easy to blame the internet for Borders'

downfall in February 2011, after an agonisingly slow death stretching over two years as store after store was closed. However, its demise was, in actual fact, far more to do with the company's complete inability to recognise what customers loved about it. Yes, a large proportion of buyers would always have defected to Amazon, but as Waterstones has subsequently proved, book buying is about so much more than simply volume and price. People are drawn to the sight, feel and smell of books. Give them this, and a large proportion will remain loyal no matter what. If only the Borders management had realised this.

STEP TWO

Get the Basics Right

Key points

- The only way for a bricks and mortar business to protect itself against the digital competition is to be unique.
- To dominate your sector, get the value equation right: quality + price + service = value.

I wouldn't want anyone to misconstrue from my earlier comments that I've downgraded the importance of getting the basics right, in other words: right products, right price, right place. This could not be further from the truth, particularly in a digital age. To be successful today, any organisation that sells anything must be highly efficient in terms of the cost of operations, which means being able to set competitive prices and being excellent at service delivery. At the same time, it is crucial to be skilled at identifying customer requirements and in curating products to meet their needs. There is also a need to 'own' the products you sell, so as not to be undercut on price or out-distributed by other online players. Last, but by no means least, there needs to be exceptional one-to-one service on offer. It's only by consistently getting these four things right that you will flourish. That's what I mean by getting the basics right.

Be Unique

In a world where Amazon sells practically everything, a retailer has to find a way to stand out. There is no point trying to compete on price or range. It's got that covered. Yet, there is one sure fire way to protect a business against the onslaught from the digital retail juggernaut: take the customer perspective, since it is the customer that is fuelling the relentless growth. And, above all, be unique.

What is it about your business that can be the point of difference?

For a start, I would put a great deal of focus on own brand. Done well, a branding that is entirely unique to a particular store can be very powerful. Waitrose's

Essentials range is a good example. When we launched in 2009, the threat in question was not Amazon, but a double whammy of a crippling recession and many of our customers switching to discounters such as Aldi and Lidl. One of the most frustrating parts of the problem was that the store was perceived to be far more expensive than its high street rivals, such as Tesco and Sainsbury's. Even though we could demonstrate price matches with hundreds of products, people just didn't seem to be convinced. The obvious answer would have been to advertise ourselves out of trouble, hit the press with a barrage of adverts and hope that some of it stuck. In my view, that was a pretty hit and miss idea though, with a low chance of success. I saw little chance that it would solve the core problem that our customers thought we were not good value.

Instead, we took the decision to do a complete rebranding of our own-brand ranges. We had a number of own label ranges at the time, but we wanted them to have a uniform, unique look and make our tiering clearer to customers. At the time, it was one of the biggest decisions in the history of Waitrose. For years we had traded on our hard won quality credentials. By completely repositioning our own brand, we risked alienating our loyal customers who might be dismayed that we'd made some sort of U-turn into 'down-market' ranges. Our research had long shown that our customers liked the store just as it was.

Our big idea was to avoid terms such as 'economy' or 'basics' for our new own-brand, and instead create a new brand called Essentials, which still emphasised quality, rather than purely price. The design for the branding with a plain white, uncluttered background was elegant and simple, which fitted in with Waitrose itself.

The launch was a huge success, with Waitrose ending 2009 as the UK's fastest growing supermarket, and Essentials contributing £121 million of incremental growth. Our customers were happy.

The second most crucial element of being unique is, well, to be truly unique. Essentials was only ever available from Waitrose and its partner online delivery service, Ocado. If a retailer goes to the trouble of creating its own brand, it should be the only outlet to sell it. In other words, it should not also be sold via Amazon or any other online or physical store. Exclusivity is key. Perhaps an even stronger example was our decision to acquire the Duchy Originals brand from the Prince of Wales. The arrangement we struck was unique, taking a licence to sell the brand with the Prince's share going to his charities, but rebranding it as Duchy Originals from Waitrose so it was only available in Waitrose. It couldn't have its value undercut online or elsewhere. It was a unique product, uniquely sold via one retailer.

Thirdly, I recommend becoming the master of curation. By this I mean managing the content and product selection for quality and compatibility with the retailer's brand that reflects your target customers, and ensuring your service and marketing reflects that curation. If a store is targeting wealthy customers, or teenagers, or technology geeks, everything it does and sells must reflect that. Retailers must be entirely innovative in the products being sold, the interior design of the store, visual merchandising, and with any add-on offers such as restaurants and cafes. A good example is Liberty London. It is 100 per cent about ethnic and avant-garde, right down to the artwork on the walls and the food it sells in its eateries. Meanwhile, Selfridges is unashamedly upscale and John Lewis is all about being the place to go to if you want to buy something reliable for your home. The White Company and Charles Tyrwhitt are two more examples of great curation. Any store that takes the old-fashioned approach of just selling loads of brands that are commonly available, hasn't got a hope. People will just go to Amazon or elsewhere online and buy the same things for less.

Meanwhile, of course, stores need to perform the juggling act of continually reinforcing to their target customers that they are focused on them and understand their needs in everything they do.

Don't Forget Value

For many years now, I have been fortunate enough to stay at the Goring Hotel in central London. It's not cheap, but the price is justified by the quality of what they offer. Yes the food and environment are excellent, but it is the service that makes the value of this hotel really sing. I prefer still to sparkling water and always sleep on the right-hand side of the bed. The team at the Goring have noticed and so always turn down the side of the bed I sleep in and put a bottle of still water on the right-hand bedside cabinet. I've never told them to do this. They just noted my habits and remembered them. When curiosity finally got the better of me and I asked about it, I was told that the hotel keeps a note of its guests' preferences from previous stays to ensure they feel at home. That is how to create true value and keep customers coming back.

Rather than thinking about right product, right price, right place, I always preferred to think about the 'value equation' when it came to getting the basics right. Sadly, these days, many interpret the word value as meaning cheap. One supermarket even has a 'value' entry-level range. It makes me wonder what that says about everything else they sell. Does it mean that it is not of value?

To clarify the true meaning of value, it is best summed up by this equation: quality + price + service = value. Just because Waitrose introduced a less expensive entry-level range called 'Essentials' did not mean that its top-end ranges were poor value for money. Far from it. All Waitrose's ranges represent value in their own way, according to the equation.

Why is value important? Well, success comes from

giving customers better value than your competitors. You can have the best service in the world, but you will not win, or keep, customers if your prices are high and your quality is poor!

Say, for instance, a can of ubiquitous Heinz Baked Beans is commonly sold for 50p. It would take quite exceptional service indeed for you to repeatedly buy your beans from a shop that sells those same beans for £1.00. As a convenience maybe, but not on a regular basis. Even then, it would be a push. In my estimation, great service might allow you to charge up to a 5 per cent premium.

The art behind achieving great sales is to constantly adjust your equation of value in response to customers' changing needs and the actions of your competitors. If you can *match* quality and price to what is going on elsewhere, but also offer better *service*, you'll win. If you are *better* on two, or even all three, of the metrics then you will be market dominant. It is easily said, but very hard to do, and hence most organisations usually make trade offs between the three. To gain comparability and then advantage in one, two or three of the value attributes means having to invest. If you're not winning now that either means raising capital to invest, reprioritising, finding additional efficiency, or all three. Once you start to win, you can keep reinvesting back from the scale growth you generate and the further efficiencies that can help to bring.

One of the businesses that I believe gets the value equation just right is Fortnum and Mason. No one walking into one of its stores would ever mistake it for another. It is unique in every way. It has a value formula that has seen it grow rapidly through an economically challenged decade in spite of trading at the top end.

In terms of quality of product, price and service, it is spot on. From its carefully curated high-quality product range to its well-laid-out interiors, it has a strongly defined point of view. The retailer knows its customers buy into its Britishness. That is why its branded hampers are famous the world over, and it works with more than 1,000 suppliers throughout the country, from bakers to butchers to chocolatiers, to ensure a unique shopping experience. Their products are certainly not cheap, but they are delicious and the environment and the service exquisite.

The Fortnum's experience begins before customers even walk inside the store: the constantly changing external window displays are frequently dressed by well-known theatre designers and you can count on them to be imaginative. Inside, the goods are laid out in a way that invites exploration and excitement at finding goods you may not have been looking for, but just *have* to buy. This is how to keep customers coming back time and again. They appreciate Fortnum and Mason's value and values.

It's in the Telling

Once a business clearly understands what matters to its customers, it needs to be precise about how that standard is achieved and measured, so that it can be communicated to the team that needs to deliver this ideal. It really is all in the telling of your business's particular story.

I once asked a manager of a gift department what his standard was for that department. In a segment like this it is, of course, essential that these areas are attractively presented for customers because they need to feel confident and excited about the gifts they choose. It is a key part of the service offering.

'To be neat and tidy,' the manager replied confidently.

Yet, on this particularly busy day before Christmas, the department was anything but.

'What does that mean?' I pressed.

At this, the manager could only shrug his shoulders. He clearly had no idea. I challenged him that if he couldn't explain to me what 'neat and tidy' meant, how on earth could his team achieve this standard, let alone allow their performance to be measured?

We then broke it down and agreed that empty baskets should be piled no higher than the cash desk. In addition, the cash desk should always be free of unsold stock, which should be taken back to its fixture. Carrier bags should be kept under the counter, not flung about on top, while tissue paper should be in one crisp pile. Waste bins should be emptied when full, empty shelves should be filled and messy fixtures should be straightened. Once we got that straight, the department had a new lease of life.

Once you are clear about the basic elements of service that customers value, and have defined how to achieve and measure them, that is when the challenge really begins.

Consistency is key. What makes companies brilliant at customer service is achieving the desired standard day in, day out. And, when it does go wrong (and it will), being brilliant in recovery.

Get the Basics Right – Winner

Harrods

Harrods is a brand that is recognised the world over and in everyone's eyes it stands for luxurious, British goods, delivered with great service that appeals to all the senses. The distinctive Knightsbridge flagship store has 1 million square feet of space, with 330 different departments. When people visit, their expectations are high.

Harrod's 4,000 full-time employees, who are supported by an additional 3,500 agency and concessionary staff, have a pivotal role to play in upholding and delivering the brand values. They're the public face of the company and each responsible for interacting with hundreds of people every day. It is, therefore, no small wonder that the shop has set such store on employee engagement. It must be doing pretty well too, since the company has been named a UK 'Top Employer' six years in a row, as well as LinkedIn's top company of 2017 and a Glassdoor 'Best Employer' for 2017.

The changes that led to Harrods' success with its team were rooted in 2006, when the retailer became alarmed at a high turnover of staff, high levels of absenteeism and a number of employee relations cases blamed on bad management practices. After conducting an extensive survey to find out what had gone wrong, the retailer decided to make changes in three areas. The first was to work at the emotional connection employees had with the famous brand. Next, they looked at economic aspects, such as pay, benefits, gender equality and career opportunities. Finally, the functional aspect of what it was actually like to work at the store were considered. What was the 'Harrods Way'?

One of the interesting things that came out of the exercise was a realisation that the annual employee surveys that were being carried out in a bid to gauge employee engagement, happiness and overall well-being, were actually having a detrimental effect. Staff members were saving up their feedback for the once a year survey, which meant that things were missed throughout the year. In response, an employee forum called Your Voice was created. The forum, made up of 140 employees from across the business, meets quarterly. It focuses on everything from employee restaurant facilities to holidays to broader business decisions on what brands to get in-store, company perception and culture.

Each day begins with a morning briefing in every department, where the floor teams are told about what is going on that day and given the latest sales statistics. An internal magazine, *Your Harrods*, features a list of new starters, interviews with key people, personal snapshots and even an agony aunt column. Everyone is encouraged to take part in the Bright Ideas scheme, which encourages the sharing of innovative ideas to further improve Harrods.

There are many programmes to promote employee growth and career progression and the Learning and Development team offers training and accredited educational opportunities. There are even internal, employee-led careers weeks with offers of coaching, placements and secondments.

Since 2007, Harrods has enjoyed double-digit

growth, and this has been put down to the focus on all of its employees, which in turn delivers an excellent customer experience. There have been noticeable improvements in customer feedback since the turn-around began. Complaints have dropped by 55 per cent, and where before customers typically left around 2,000 praise or recommendation comments each year, now that number is nearer 11,000. Labour turnover has halved from 48 per cent ten years ago, to 22 per cent, which is a good figure in London where there is traditionally a high employee turnover rate. Absenteeism is down to the lowest rate in the sector, and stability, or the amount of time employees stay with a store for over two years, is at 75 per cent.

The ultimate proof of success is that the culture of Harrods has changed and everyone there feels that they have played a role in the improvement. The team is proud to live up to the values reflected by the Harrods brand, and this is reflected in how they behave. Their contribution gives the luxury store a competitive edge and ensures it maintains its reputation as one of the world's most luxurious retailers.

GET THE BASICS RIGHT – LOSER

Comet

Electrical retailer Comet began life in Yorkshire in 1933 when it was known as Comet Battery Stores and offered a service recharging batteries for customers' radios. It first opened its doors as a bona fide retailer in the fifties, buoyed by the boom in electrical products. It did, however, remain predominantly a mail order business, selling stock at prices up to 45 per cent lower than its competition. Growth was steady over the years, in line with the public's appetite for white goods, TVs and other electrical products, and arguably Comet kept pace with it. There were precious few bells and whistles as far as customer service was concerned, but trading on its cheapest-on-the-high-street credentials seemed to work OK.

Right up until it stopped working.

When US giant Wal-Mart took over Asda in 1999 the move wiped close to £700 million off the value of UK chain stores. The announcement that the American chain would be discounting some electrical goods by 60 per cent shook the City. And no doubt the Comet board were very aware that their store was somewhat of a one trick pony. To survive, Comet had to at least match some of Wal-Mart's discounts, but to grow at all they had to do something even better than their new, deep-pocketed rival.

Searching around for a solution, Comet rebranded. Customers had long confused Comet with its rival Dixons, since they both had white logos on a red background, so the reasoning was, make the store different and the customer will come back, right? Wrong. Despite a £20 million rebranding exercise, customers were not convinced that Comet presented a unique opportunity. Comet continued to lose market share.

To add to the already mounting pressure, online rivals began making inroads into Comet's traditional heartland: mail order. Although Comet also sold via the internet, it was now just one of dozens of electrical stores. It had no USP, since everyone was offering keen prices.

The final straw was the economic crash that began in 2007. Consumers tightened their belts as wages were frozen, unemployment rose and the property market stalled. Discretionary purchases collapsed.

By this stage, Comet was running out of options. Since it operated in a fiercely competitive market with cripplingly low margins, it was never going to be able to sustain a cost leadership position. Latest products, such as LED TVs, sell at a premium in the first year, but prices almost halve annually after that. Retailers have to sell double the volume just to keep up. Competing on price is the hardest strategy of all in this market. Yet, Comet still relentlessly focused on price.

Meanwhile, with no cash to spare, the in-store experience suffered markedly. The stores lacked investment and became lacklustre and shabby. Many of them were on grim, underinvested, first generation out-of-town retail parks. Customers were more likely to find a burger van outside than a Starbucks. Hardly an inspiring shopping experience.

Staff numbers were kept to a minimum with apparent complete disregard of the fact that it is essential to inspire customers when shopping for electrical products. Plus, of course, there is a need for information, advice and reassurance. When there is little or no attempt to create a unique personal relationship, it is easy to fall victim to showrooming, which is where people visit the high street to touch and look at product up close, then go home and order it online. Interestingly, Dixons, the competitor Comet was so keen to differentiate itself from by rebranding, invested vast sums on staff training and a 'Knowhow' programme. It recognised that the one thing bricks and mortar retailers could do that would make them stand out from online stores was to offer solid face-to-face advice and guidance.

The final nail in the coffin, customer-wise, was the extended warranties Comet tried so hard to sell. These were an epidemic post-millennium. Basically, customers who had made the decision to buy a particular item were then given a very hard sell to buy a three-year extended warranty, in case their shiny new product broke (as it probably will, sir/madam) in the intervening years. What a terrible message to give a customer! Not only did this add up to 40 per cent or more onto the price, it was also a complete sham. Customers automatically have certain legal rights if a product doesn't perform as expected or breaks under normal usage. Even if there was some accidental damage that wouldn't be covered in this way, household insurance may well cover it. However, with store staff heavily incentivised to sell the warranties, the practice continued unabated. Comet were not the only retailer guilty of this, but with little else to excite customers, it really shot itself in the foot here.

Comet entered administration in November 2012, prompting the closure of 240 stores.

STEP THREE

Create the Perfect Customer Journey

Key Points

- Visualise your customer journey, every step of the way. Take each step and imagine: how do we make this customer experience better?
- Take the time to remind customers that they have made a great decision in their choice of product and, of course, buying it from you.

One of the main things that I used to be obsessive about at Waitrose was the customer journey. I spent hours and hours visualising everyone's shopping trip, every step of the way. I did this time after time because I was always keen to find ways to improve it. Where were the opportunities to create that connection and add to their happiness? What had I missed?

To me, that journey began before a customer had left

the comfort of their own home; indeed long before they even contemplated their trip to the supermarket. There had to be a way (or ways) to put Waitrose and its products at the top of their minds. One of the answers we favoured was to produce an assortment of beautiful (branded) recipe cards, which we gave away free. We knew people collected them and would pull them out to make their favourite dishes and there the name Waitrose would be, branded on top of the card. Another good way to keep us top of mind was our glossy magazine that was filled with delicious recipes, including inspirational ideas of what to cook every day of the week, often with a seasonal theme and, hopefully, left lying in the kitchen. Branded reusable bags (before they were legally required) and reusable Waitrose-branded cups all, I hoped, put the thought of going to Waitrose for your shopping top of mind.

My focus then moved on to what customers might experience when they arrived for their shopping trip. Were our car parks easy to navigate, spotlessly clean, with spaces wide enough for even the largest family cars? And, very importantly, could the driver easily get out of their car once they parked? I wanted our trolleys to be quick to locate and make sure that there was always a good selection of different sizes. It was important they were all clean too. No one likes a dirty trolley or to be faced with the detritus from the previous shopper's exertions. I knew from experience there needed to be a towel or cloth handy, so if for any reason the trolleys became damp or dirty, customers would be able to wipe them. Parents of young children in particular valued this service since trolleys with inbuilt child seats can accumulate a mass of interesting titbits.

After that, I visualised the shopper's journey to the front of the shop. In many stores today, one of the first things a customer sees is a large, unfriendly-looking security guard standing at the entrance. Chances are, his arms will be folded across his chest and he'll be staring at each shopper in a challenging way as they enter the store. That's not exactly a welcoming sight is it? Just to make the atmosphere that little bit more hostile, there may even be posters on the sliding doors, sporting mug shots of whoever has been banned from the store for some misdemeanour, and a large CCTV camera may well be recording you entering the shop. There may also be posters warning about products that have been recalled for some defect or another. Again, not exactly enticing. You are going shopping, not about to make an appearance at Crown Court.

As a preference, Waitrose places cut flowers all around the front entrances. (On the rare occasions a security guard is present, they maintain a more discrete presence.) We knew the average Waitrose customer is most likely a keen gardener or greatly interested in nature. Moving the fresh flowers right to the entrance of the store, with plants outside that so these are the first things people see when they arrive was therefore an easy improvement to make. Not only does it make the stores seem less institutional, but it also greatly increased our sales of cut flowers and plants. They also reinforce seasonality – so important in fresh-food retailing. We also installed welcome desks just beyond the fresh flowers. Colleagues greet each customer as they go through with a smile. How much better is this than a uniformed guard looking you up and down?

There are dozens of opportunities to add just a little extra to a customer's shopping experience by focusing on their journey through the store too. Benches were added so anyone who is tired with shopping or not able to accompany their partner all the way around the store, can rest awhile. There are also the coffee and papers I have already mentioned.

When it comes to the goods sold, everything was made easily accessible, with self-service bags left in obvious places so customers didn't have to hunt around for them. If a customer needed to to weigh or label something themselves, we made sure they didn't need a degree in computer science just to work the machine – one, maybe two, obvious and very quick steps would be sufficient.

If experts are appropriate for a particular department: we provided them. We put wine experts in the drinks section because wine is a big purchase and a lot of customers aren't always sure what they want to buy. We also put trained experts on the meat and fish counters to help customers by preparing meat and fish and giving tips on how to cook it. Likewise for fruit and vegetables. Whenever there was a chance to encourage a customer to try and taste a product we would take it – in wine and beer, on the deli counter, even on packaged goods. Treats galore as you wander the store were also encouraged. We made our aisles wider and our top shelves lower to make the shopping experience more comfortable.

The biggest bugbear of any shopping trip anywhere is what happens when you are done: the queue to pay. This is the experience that can make or break what a customer thinks of your store. Imagine the change of attitude after someone has (hopefully) enjoyed everything about their visit to your shop, spent 15 minutes or half an hour gathering all they want to buy, and then are confronted with a ten minute queue, just to pay for it. Stand by any checkout and watch the reaction of customers when they see a queue. Their shoulders visibly slump.

Careful management of the cashier process is crucial. Cash desk 101 is making sure there are enough cashiers available to keep things moving. Then you need to get down to the details. Timing is key. Waitrose cashiers are trained to start *only after* the customer has unloaded everything onto the belt. That way, the customer can move to the other end and start packing, without feeling they are in a stressful race against the cashier. Similarly, a cashier matches scanning the goods to the pace that a customer is packing. Again, it makes people very tense when they see their purchases piling up in front of them in a disorganised and growing pile as they race to keep up.

The cash desk offers endless opportunities to reinforce a customer's good feeling about their shopping experience. The handing-over of payment is another key point. If a customer pays by cash, the cashier should put the change in their hand, not leave it in a pile on the side so they have to scoop it up. If a card payment is made, it costs nothing for a cashier to take the card and put it in the machine and afterwards thank the customer by name.

'Thank you Mr Smith,' is so much better than a card silently handed over as the cashier dismissively turns to their next customer.

The whole process of the care, the pace, the speed and the kindness with which a cashier treats you, makes a huge difference to whether a shopper favours one place or another.

It doesn't do any harm to finish the journey with something that makes customers feel good about themselves either. The relationship shouldn't just end abruptly because the customer has handed over their money and is on the way out. After all, don't forget, the aim should be to value the customer you have. The cashier will ask the customer if they would like their free cup of tea or coffee and newspaper if they haven't taken it already. And this was partly why I introduced the Waitrose Community Matters scheme. At the end of each trip shoppers are given a green token to place in the box of the good cause they'd most like to support. The more tokens a cause gets, the bigger the donation from Waitrose. In its first decade since its launch in 2008, more than £14 million was donated to more than 38,000 local charities chosen by customers. Customers love the scheme because they are doing something positive for the community and they feel great about that. It's the perfect, feel good way to round off an enjoyable and painless shopping trip. And the added bonus is customers encouraging their friends to shop to support this charity or that. I heard of a church group being featured for a month, and so the vicar in his Sunday sermon encouraged all the congregation to shop at Waitrose!

When you visualise the customer journey, everything is viewed through the lens of how do we make this customer experience right?

What Does Great Service Look Like for My Customers?

I've talked a lot about the journey of the Waitrose customer, from home to store and back again. Clearly, though, a customer will expect a very different experience if they, say, go clothes shopping or to buy a big item of furniture for their home. And this is key: each and every retailer offers a very different journey for their customers, or at least they *should* do. The tools at their disposal to make people feel happy about their shopping trip vary wildly. There is no one-size-fits-all when it comes to customer happiness.

If you sell anything and want to know how to make your buyers smile, you need to go through a process that questions what great service looks like for the individuals who buy from you. My suggestion would be to go through that journey yourself, step by step, so you can better understand what it is a customer really expects in your unique case.

Take, as an example, a retailer selling cards and gifts. What does great service look like when a customer wants to buy someone a birthday card? The customer most likely wants to pop into the shop for just a few moments, possibly because they are on the way somewhere else or on their lunch hour. They'll want to be able to quickly find and choose a card. In fact, speed is of the essence, because it is not the only purchase they'll be making that day and possibly not the most important, either. In an ideal world, all the cards will be grouped together and clearly labelled by occasion: birthdays, anniversaries, condolences, and so on. Subdivisions of the categories, such as birthday wishes for close relatives, men, women or children, should also be easy to spot. The designs should be laid out in a way that makes it simple and quick for the customer to find what they are looking for.

Once again, the queuing experience (or lack of queuing) is as crucial, if not more crucial than in a supermarket. No one is in the mood to wait even a couple of minutes to buy a £2 card. Nor should they be expected to. Neither do they want to engage with the cashier to discuss what a nice design the birthday card is, who it is for and whether or not 70-years old is a great age to be. Customers just want to pay and leave.

Therefore, great service in a card shop is a well-laid-out store so the customer is able to find something quickly and easily, and an efficient payment service. Price is not really a determinant. That's the basic level required to make a customer happy.

Contrast the card store experience with what a customer might expect when buying a designer jacket at a high-end clothes shop. If someone is going to pay hundreds of pounds for a single item, they want a completely different level of service. For now, let's take the exclusive environment, layout and tidiness of the store for granted. The vital factor in this experience is the interaction between the shop staff and the customer. The level of service required is highly personal. A customer needs an attentive assistant who will help them choose the right garment, talk knowledgeably about the various options and guide them towards the most flattering choice. Once that choice has been made, there needs to be a level of positive reinforcement where the shop assistant reassures the customer they have made a very astute decision and look fantastic in the chosen jacket. The attention to detail continues to the till (where there is no queue, naturally) and the sales assistant either deals with the purchase themselves or warmly hands the customer over to a colleague. The jacket is not then stuffed into a carrier bag after the payment is taken, but instead lovingly folded and packaged between layers of fine tissue, put into a branded bag and the bag sealed with a bow. Before the customer leaves the store, the final words they will hear is another bit of reinforcement that they are wonderful and perhaps even an invitation to be added to the customer database so they can be invited to the champagne launch of the next season's collection. The subtext: You, dear customer, are amazing!

Different shop, different product, entirely different customer journey.

In another scenario, imagine our customer now wants to buy a laptop and takes themselves off to a high street department store or electronics outlet. This person is about to spend upwards of £1,000 on this important purchase. In this case, the shop assistant also plays a crucial role. However, the perfect customer journey here relies on the assistant being extremely knowledgeable and well versed in everything to do with the products in question. Customers (quite rightly) expect adequate time to be devoted to fully understanding their exact requirements, which means assistants must devote time and energy to getting to know their needs. The smoothness of the customer journey depends upon the assistant getting up to speed with what's needed by asking a series of incisive questions:

'How often will you be using this laptop?'

'Can you describe the sort of work you'll be using it for?'

'Is it being used in connection with other technology you already have?'

'What are the requirements regarding memory on the machine?'

Then, having gathered all the information, there is an expectation of an informed, well-considered and fair recommendation.

'This machine is fantastic value for £999, but for what you've just described you need, I believe you may be better off with this one. The good news is it is £100 cheaper.'

In this circumstance, great service is so much more than having the right products, at the right price, at the right time. The icing on the cake that will make a customer feel they have gone to the right place is the fact they have spent time with someone who is super-knowledgeable about that product. You don't need anyone to be super-knowledgeable when you are buying your designer jacket. The designer store assistant's primary role is to be supremely charming (along with having a feeling for fashion too, naturally). You don't need someone who is super-knowledgeable when you buy a greetings card: you just need fast and efficient service.

There are certain purchases where 'great service' is nothing to do with what happens at the point of purchase. What makes a customer happy is that they are relaxed about what will happen next. For this, imagine a business to business transaction like, say, buying a Rolls-Royce engine for an aeroplane. This is, of course, a major investment which can stretch over years allowing for the negotiation, waiting list and installation time. In this case, let's take it as a given that the product will be top quality, will work perfectly and will come in at a competitive price. The customer can rest assured on these counts. The part of the customer journey that Rolls-Royce needs to focus on is making sure the customer feels confident that the firm will be around for the next 20 years or so for all the specialised maintenance that will be required. Much needs to be made of the top-notch, highly trained engineers that will be on call every step of the way, perpetually keeping those engines in the best possible condition and the planes they power in the air. The customer must be satisfied that following the sale, everything will continue to a very high standard.

The one customer journey we definitely cannot ignore today is the digital one. Online sales are increasing by double figures each year, and 87 per cent of UK consumers have bought at least one product online in the last 12 months.[2] The most common purchases are electronics and digital media, including video games, music downloads, e-books, computers and phones, with the fashion industry coming in a close second, accounting for almost a third of our online buying. When it comes to grocery, my former business, to date 48 per cent of people have bought their groceries online and 11 per cent claim to do the majority of their food shopping via the web.

[2] Office for National Statistics, March 2017.

Like all the other journeys documented here, Customer expectations around the digital journey are unique and specific.

Once again, there are (or should be) a number of aspects of the shopping experience that are a given. Every retailer's website should work ultra smoothly and be easy to navigate. Customers should be able to find the required item/s and then checkout in a simple, uncomplicated manner. Ditto, the price level should be competitive, especially since comparison with a rival service is but one click away.

When it comes to customer happiness in digital purchases, the number one consideration is that the goods are delivered when they said they will be delivered and arrive exactly as described. Customers need to have the confidence that the goods can be returned if not right. This is great service in the digital context. A customer needs to be 100 per cent confident they'll get what they paid for in the virtual world, just as they would if they went and picked it up themselves in the real world. Start imposing hefty delivery charges and then dither and delay on getting the goods to the customer, and a digital store is on a slippery slope.

Good service starts with getting the basics right. That's not as easy as it might sound, and my starting point would always be to follow the journey of your individual customer base and to work out what is important to them. What does the product or service being sold look like from their point of view? What might worry or distract them if you don't get it quite right? Put it into context right from the moment they first imagine making a purchase, even if they have not left the comfort of their home or workplace.

Cognitive Dissonance Reduction

There was something I touched on in the previous section that I would like to develop further here. In the designer-jacket-buying scenario I mentioned how important it was that the customer is told that they've made a great choice. It reaffirms their decision when they might be having a slight wobble about buying such a costly, non-essential item, and perhaps something different to what they might have intended. However, while it is especially important in that sort of scenario, I do believe that there is a lot to be said for this sort of interaction in many other circumstances.

The technical term for it is 'cognitive dissonance reduction', which isn't very snappy or memorable, I grant you. It's that uncomfortable feeling of holding contradictory views, ideas or values, particularly with reference to a long-held belief that is challenged by new evidence to the contrary. In a retail context however, what is well worth remembering is that we all need a little reassurance, particularly when we are spending our hard-earned money. Did I choose the right retailer to buy from? The right brand? The right colour and fit? The right price?

I started thinking about this many years ago, when I was still working at John Lewis. Many of our customers were making some quite substantial purchases, and I knew that while they were in-store, they were getting all the help and encouragement you might expect from our well-trained, highly engaged colleagues. But what happened when they left the store and got home after spending a considerable amount of money? I was quite sure that at least some of our customers engaged in a spot of 'buyer's remorse', wondering if they might have done better elsewhere. *Should I have shopped around more? Did I get the best deal?*

I started a trial at our Cheadle store where, after a customer made a significant purchase of a TV or white goods, such as a washing machine, a colleague would telephone the following day or shortly after the item in question had been delivered.

They'd ask: 'Has your TV/washing machine/ dishwasher been delivered OK?'

Then, after the customer had confirmed all was in order, they would follow up with:

'That is great news. You made an excellent purchase there. That machine is just right for what you wanted and it is on at a good price at the moment.'

Or perhaps:

'That manufacturer's only bringing out that model for a short amount of time. You're smart to buy it now.'

Once more, it all goes back to loving the customer you have. Can you imagine how reassuring it is to be told you've made a great choice? I am surprised how few companies even consider what is a relatively simple thing to do. Simple, but hugely effective.

I should add, there are limits to how far you should go in respect of cognitive dissonance reduction. Thanks to the digital age, it is very easy to be in constant touch with customers, but it is possible to overdo it and totally wreck what was previously a very pleasant customer journey. I am sure many people can relate to an experience I had not that long ago. I bought a pair of very smart shoes from an established store. I'd spent a little more on them than I usually would have done, but reasoned that they were well worth the investment since I was then covering a lot of mileage on foot in my job as a Trade Minister. I had high hopes they would outlast my previous, cheaper pairs.

I smiled to myself when the cashier asked me for my email address. I assumed that this upmarket store was well up on the idea of cognitive dissonance reduction and was planning to follow up at a later date by asking how I was getting on with my pricey new shoes. Perhaps, they might even offer a complimentary resoling service in a few years' time. After all, these shoes were designed to last many years.

This was not what happened at all. My interaction with the store unleashed a veritable barrage of emails with the most inane marketing messages. What's more, they were completely irrelevant to me. After a short time I got totally fed up with the store and unsubscribed from their email list. I was doubly frustrated by what had happened. The emails were annoying and intrusive, but what was more aggravating was that they had totally missed the point of focusing on the customer's point of view. It would have cost them virtually nothing to send an email saying something on the lines of: how are those shoes fitting? Or, are they wearing in nicely? If they had done so, I wouldn't have baulked if they'd followed up with, you bought those shoes, here are some more you might like. As it was, I shall never shop there again. It was a thoroughly disappointing experience.

It is very easy to hide behind technology, imagining you are in constant touch with your customers. However, are you talking to them or at them? More and more I see evidence of the latter.

CREATE THE PERFECT CUSTOMER JOURNEY – WINNER

Topshop

There was a time when if you walked into an average high street fashion store on a busy day, you'd be forgiven for thinking you had entered hell on earth. Chances are the layout would be confusing and chaotic, the changing rooms hard to find and crowded and there wouldn't be any staff nearby to help. There was one chain that, to my mind, changed the tone in getting everything about the customer journey right though: Topshop. Specifically, Topshop's flagship store in London's Oxford Street. Although the Arcadia group has now fallen on more controversial times, at one point the chain was getting the customer experience just right, and this is sure to be emulated and remembered by retailers in years to come.

This store has everything a young, and indeed old, fashionista could desire, and that in itself is one of its achievements. It has a broad appeal and there is something to surprise and delight anyone interested in the latest clothing trends. Whether it is celebrity ranges from Kate Moss and Beyoncé, or boutique, vintage or leisure collections, what is on offer appeals to all tastes and pockets. In fact, it has been called a hotbed of discovery, with lots of different areas to inspire customers, which is exactly what it should be.

The idea behind it is to take the store beyond being a simple clothing outfit where customers can browse for a new dress or T-shirt. Topshop cleverly takes them on a journey that tempts them with all sorts of other things they might not even realise they wanted while browsing in-store. Thus, alongside a slick personal shopping operation, which is free of charge, there is a number of hair and beauty services, ranging from brow shaping to piercing. You could even get a tattoo if you want one. Rubbing shoulders with these temptations are brightly lit and innovative integrated food and drink pop-ups, such as Bubbleology and Lola's Cupcakes, which ensure that shoppers can relax and refresh themselves before jumping back into the fray. There are also photo booths for the all-important group pictures with friends.

Much is made of newness; in other words, regular customers know that if they visit on any day, they will always discover something new. Hundreds of new designs are introduced each week.

Everywhere you look, the emphasis is on the unexpected, which is another thing that differentiates this store from many of its chain-store rivals that change clothes with the seasons, but not much else. There are regular switches between retail brand pop-ups and giant video walls screening the latest fashion shows. It's interactive too. In 2017, Topshop's window displays were turned into an interactive pool scene. Customers were invited to ride a virtual water slide before being taken off on a virtual reality journey across Oxford Street. Cue lots of water-slide selfies on social media, spreading the word still further. Another time, the entire store was pumped with the scent of sun lotion and a special Topshop Snapchat filter created for social sharing.

Thought has been given to personalising the journey too. Each customer is an individual, and if they want their clothes to reflect that, it is possible: there is a service to embroider or patch denims in any design the customer likes.

Topshop has made great strides in making the customer journey an exciting, interactive event that people want to share with friends. Much thought has been given to how to ensure customers spend time in-store so they can fully engage with the brand and be inspired by what is on offer. Without a doubt, the customer journey has certainly reflected a brand that prides itself on being a trendsetter.

Create the Perfect Customer Journey – Loser

Blockbuster

Blockbuster was, at one time, *the* place to be if you wanted to rent a movie to watch at home. Customers would flock to one of its more than 9,000 high street stores, manned by more than 60,000 employees and browse shelf upon shelf of Hollywood greats before taking their video, and later DVD, home for a cosy night's viewing.

As far as Blockbuster was concerned, it was riding the crest of the wave of its success as the biggest player in the market and the customer journey was clear-cut. In the company's mind, the experience movie lovers were buying was to walk into the store, pick up a movie and maybe some popcorn as a treat. Except they missed the fact that wasn't the experience customers were after at all. What they actually valued was the experience of *watching a movie*, perhaps with some popcorn too. Having a large selection of movies to choose from was important, but the act of visiting a store was a long way down the list of priorities.

Being completely oblivious to what customers valued made Blockbuster very vulnerable. As the well-told story goes, in 2000, when Reed Hastings, the founder of a fledgling company called Netflix, flew to Dallas to offer Blockbuster CEO John Antioco a partnership, he was practically laughed out of the office. Netflix's deal was that it would offer a DVD rental service but run the brand online, posting out the DVDs, while Blockbuster would promote Netflix in stores. Why would we want to do that? was Blockbuster's response.

The arrival of Lovefilm and later acquisition by Amazon, to form the genesis of their digital steaming offer, was further proof of market change.

Everyone knows what happened next: Blockbuster went bankrupt in 2010 and Netflix moved into streaming in 2007 and now dominates our small screens as a multi-billion-dollar movie company, offering films and TV shows and its own original content.

Again, it is easy to blame Blockbuster's demise on a bold digital rival or on making a cripplingly bad mistake in ignoring Netflix's overtures. There is more to it than that, though, and the misunderstanding of what customers actually wanted is at the heart of the problem.

One of the clear weaknesses in Blockbuster's business model was that it made much of its money on the back of charging its customers punitive fees for returning their rentals late. The ugly truth, which became the company's Achilles heel, was that it came to rely on this practice as a crucial revenue stream. Rather than more appropriately building a personal relationship where a customer might be congratulated on their great choice of film, *'If you enjoyed that, sir, you'll love this,'* customers were hounded to pay up if the rental was returned even a few hours later than expected. Not surprisingly, customers hated late fees.

Netflix, of course, had the advantage that since it didn't have any retail locations, it could afford to offer a greater range of movies and there was no need to rely on late fees to bolster its income. Customers could keep movies as long as they wanted too. This meant the service automatically ticked all the boxes for a customer: they could watch a movie whenever they wanted (with or without popcorn) and return it whenever they felt like it without being charged.

Netflix focused its efforts on creating a customer experience online. Even though it started life as a mail order video rental service, it pioneered providing recommendations depending upon how customers rated a film. These sort of recommendations are par for the course now, but back then they were very innovative. Netflix even offered a $1 million prize to anyone who could come up with an even better rating system. The service knew that this was what made customers tick.

As Blockbuster started to struggle, losing customers to Netflix, it continued to stoically ignore the customer journey. Spectacularly failing to read what was important to people coming into the stores, it filled its shelves with books, toys and other merchandise. Customers who were just looking to rent a great film were more turned off than ever.

Blockbuster did eventually move to introduce mail order movie rentals, and even movie streaming, but they were too slow to do so and customers had already been turned off by the shoddy way they'd been treated in the past. Netflix, which had never focused on protecting its existing revenue, had introduced online streaming as soon as it could, even though it cannibalised its mail order business. It was fleet of foot when it came to recognising the shift in customer journeys and was repaid with even greater loyalty.

While the digital market put exceptional pressure on Blockbuster, it was its inability to understand the customer journey and what customers really wanted from the experience that did for this retailer. While they were looking the wrong way entirely, a niche idea was able to snowball into one of the most successful companies in the world.

Step Four

Human Interaction

Key Points

- Staff play a huge role in customer happiness. Empower them and listen to them. They are on the front line.
- Help customers feel that you genuinely have their best interests at heart.

Picture the scene. It's a smart London restaurant and two people are deep in conversation at a table in the far corner. Both diners are wearing smart dark business suits, so it is safe to assume this is not a social event. They are most likely discussing something concerning their corporate life, whether or not they work for the same organisation or one of them acts as a supplier or adviser to another. On the table in front of them are two menus. Both are unopened.

The waiter, wearing smart black trousers, a crisp white shirt and a pristine apron, hurries over, pen and notepad poised.

'Are you ready to order, sirs?' he asks politely, breaking into the intense conversation.

Both of the diners look up and smile politely.

'No, could you give us a little while?' asks one.

The waiter nods and walks away.

Two minutes later the waiter returns. Despite the fact that both menus are still untouched, he repeats his question.

'Are you ready to order, sirs?'

Again, both diners look up and smile politely after breaking off from their conversation. If you'd have looked closely, you may have seen a trace of irritation pass over their brows.

'Not yet,' responded one. 'Can you give us more time?'

The process is repeated a further three times, at two minute intervals before the diners finally break off their conversation and quickly open and scan the menu before ordering. They then immediately revert to their discussion even as the waiter is rearranging their tableware in line with their order.

When the first course arrives, the pair acknowledge the waiter, thank him and continue to talk as they eat. Although it would be clear to any observer that they were getting along well, it was also apparent that the subject under discussion was very serious as there was little laughter accompanying their talk.

'How is that for you?' the waiter interrupts, as they are midway through their starter, and conversation.

'Fine, fine,' says one of the two, barely looking up.

The process is repeated almost word for word shortly after the main course is delivered.

During the meal there are no fewer than a dozen interruptions, asking anything from whether the dinners would like more water/bread/wine to whether they were interested in dessert/coffee or simply were enjoying what they were eating. The same question was even asked twice on a couple of occasions.

I relate this story because it was exactly what happened to me a short time ago. I was dining with the chairman of one of the UK's most successful companies. We needed to discuss a number of very serious issues and it led to a very deep conversation. What amazed me was how the staff in this very well-established restaurant totally failed to read this. No one looked at us and thought: Ah, these two obviously have things to discuss, we will keep the interruptions to a minimum. They just carried on as they did with every cover. Perhaps the waiters had been trained to do this and were following orders to the letter, in which case their training, and company policy, failed to empower then to use their initiative.

Now, I completely understand that the staff had a job to do and restaurants need to keep things moving in order to remain profitable. I also value attentive service as much as the next person, and there are plenty of times I have enjoyed leisurely lunches where I have chatted happily with the staff. However, this was not the right tactic for that particular occasion.

The reason for raising this story is because human interaction is a key part of the customer experience. Again, though, it is not a one-size-fits-all affair. Staff play a crucial role in customer happiness and this requires a level of intuition about what an individual actually needs.

In my engaging.works workplace happiness survey I ask two questions to understand how empowered individuals are to deliver great service. The first question is if the individual feels empowered. This speaks to whether company policy provides the individual with sufficient latitude to do what's required. The second is if they feel trusted to make decisions. This question gets to the heart of whether an individual's line manager supports the flexibility required to meet customers' needs.

Done well, the human touch makes all the difference between an 'OK' experience and a really pleasant one. I recently spoke with the boss of a major hotel chain who told me that when they had big functions, they used to have teams of people in the kitchens filling up trays of drinks that were then put out on tables for guests. They now use machines to do that side of things and the people who used to do the job are sent out to smile at guests as they hand out the drinks. This human touch made customers far, far happier, he explained. I have no doubts at all that it does.

Even though we are in a digital age, this is no time to hide behind technology. Sure, you can use technology to send customers offers and texts to welcome them through the doors. But, every customer knows it doesn't really mean you like them as a person and are pleased to see them back. What we all value is the human touch. A unique greeting that says: 'Hello, welcome back,' or 'How are you today?' The world is moving in a direction where it seems businesses want less contact with their customers, when actually what many people are crying out for is a bit of interaction.

The key is to get the level of interaction just right, which is not always easy when it is down to the individual.

Reading the Customer

Years ago, when I started to run the lighting department at John Lewis in Southampton, clocks were sold in the same area. Well, I say sold, but in actual fact very few were sold at all. Anyone who wished to buy one would have to locate an assistant and then wait while the glass case they were in was unlocked and the clock in question brought out for inspection.

I decided to experiment by releasing the clocks. The glass at the front of the case was removed, so any interested buyer could simply reach in and pick up a clock from the shelf to examine it. Sales shot up by 200 per cent.

This showed me that clock buyers were not interested in having a conversation. There are many instances in retail where customers simply don't have the time, energy or desire to discuss their purchases. Similarly, there are many where customers do want advice and reassurance.

To make things a little more tricky for retailers, it is often a generational thing too. I would much rather speak to a real person when I am buying a train ticket. However, my two daughters think nothing of using the machines in stations, which they find far quicker and easier to navigate.

While views on human interaction vary from situation to situation, what I see coming across very clearly is we do still need people. We have a human need to socialise and in an increasingly digital world, I can only see that need becoming stronger.

Observation is key when it comes to reading the customer. While retailers can score big customer happiness points by getting all aspects of the journey just right, the way to create a real edge is to make sure every person leaving the store believes they've been understood as an individual.

This is, of course, entirely in the hands of the people on the front line: the staff. In the example that opened this section, the restaurant ticked the right boxes in every aspect of the journey. The environment, food and welcome was spot on. Then it was all ruined because the team on the ground didn't appear to use any judgement about what the customers really wanted.

Training is key here and a basic understanding of body language.

If good service is doing exactly what the customer wants, retailers need to think what that means in their particular context. What are the signs that a customer just wants to be left alone to get on with it? Or that they feel a little lost and in need of advice? Can a sales assistant spot the irritation if a customer feels overlooked or when they have been asked the same question by several of their colleagues? How often have you tried to attract the attention of staff with a wave or a smile only to be ignored or rebuked?

Staff should certainly be encouraged to look at customers and to make a judgement about what they want and need *before* bowling in and making a suggestion that may be completely unwarranted.

This may also require a certain amount of flexibility around the customer journey. To go back to the earlier examples in Step 3, the customer journey section, in a card shop the sales assistant might intervene in the usually hands-off process if they observe a customer looking a little lost or confused. Here, it would be appropriate to say, 'Can I help you?' rather than sticking rigidly to the philosophy that it is a quick, discretionary process where customers are in and out in a matter of moments. Likewise, in the designer jacket shop, if the shopper looks like they are flustered and in a bit of a hurry, the sales assistant should cut short some of the flattery.

There is an entire industry devoted to 'reading' body language cues, where everything from the way someone folds their arms, to whether or not their pupils dilate, all have a very definite meaning. There is no need to go into this depth in a retail situation where untold numbers of people may be walking into a shop in any given day.

However, staff can be encouraged to look out for key indicators of individual shopper's mood. It is easy to determine from most people's expressions if they are surprised, dissatisfied, confused or hesitant. If a customer is avoiding eye contact and moving at a pace, they most likely don't want to be stopped and asked if they need help. If they are standing still and scratching their head, then they are probably lost and confused. It is therefore time to step in and ask if they need assistance. If someone stops a member of the team and actually asks for help, then the assistant should engage to whatever degree appears to be required, rather than pointing them off in a vague direction.

It's also worth noting that a salesperson's body language is equally telling. Constantly checking a mobile phone rather than attending to customers is an obvious no-no. Customers will notice the body language of staff from the moment they enter a store and, as everyone knows, first impressions count. Everyone likes to be greeted by a smile and a hello. It sets the tone for the entire visit. Staff that are not in the closest proximity to the store entrance (and therefore not involved in the greeting) should not be slumped over the till or standing in groups talking to one another. It sends a very negative message.

Eye contact is crucial, but getting the right amount can be tricky. No one wants to feel like they are being stared down by shop staff or ignored. The happy medium is maintaining enough eye contact to show that they are interested in the customer and happy to talk/help out as required. Similarly, the team should remain visible at all times and look like they are ready to help, but not hover over the customer. This can be off-putting and make them feel like they are being watched.

It certainly helps if the team is genuinely interested, and I shall talk about this further in Step Six – Empowering the Team.

—————— **Impartiality and Transparency** ——————

I'm going to make a bit of a confession here (another one!). One of my guilty pleasures is watching a programme on Sky TV called *American Pickers*. If you have never heard of it, let me enlighten you. It features two men, Mike Wolfe and Frank Fritz, who travel across the US, looking for Americana. If they find artefacts and national treasures they like, they either buy them to sell on in antiques shops or add them to their personal collections. They travel all over the place, often scrabbling around neglected barns or dusty spare rooms to find their prize.

Once Mike and Frank find what they like, they'll negotiate with the rightful owner. A little haggling will ensue, but they always seem quite fair and pay pretty close to what the owner asks for. Every so often though, they'll ask the owner how much they want for the object and the owner will come back with a price of, say, $100.

'I think it is worth a lot more than that,' will come the surprise response from Mike or Frank. 'This is worth $200.'

Then they will give the no-doubt delighted seller the higher price.

I really like it when they do this. It's not just great TV, it is also a perfect example of how transparency gives you the edge with customers. People value honesty like this (who wouldn't?) and inevitably the delighted owner tells the two treasure customers to come back again any time they like. At a stroke, a potential long-term relationship has been created.

As a child, I had exactly the opposite experience, so I know first-hand how much it burns to regret a transaction that is blatantly unfair. I had a stamp collection that was handed down to me by my mother's father. I wasn't particularly interested in being a philatelist, so decided that I would sell it and spend the money on something that was of more interest to me. I took myself off to the nearest town centre, where I knew there was a shop that bought and sold stamps and went in and offered my collection to the owner. He leafed through the book and sucked in his cheeks a bit as though pondering on a price.

'I'll give you £10,' he said at last.

It was a lot of money to a child, but I was a bit disappointed nonetheless. He must have seen my hesitation, because he flicked through the book again and upped his offer.

'All right, I'll give you £20,' he said. 'There are one or two good ones in here.'

A while later, when I mentioned the incident in passing to relatives, I discovered that there were some really valuable stamps in that collection. The shop owner had completely, and I have no doubt knowingly, ripped me off. I was utterly furious and devastated too. In fact, I have never forgotten it.

Businesses need to think hard about what is genuinely best for each customer if they want them to be happy. This means they may have to think carefully about the incentives and sales targets they give to their teams.

While sales incentives are an important part of any retail operation, if they are pegged to the performance of individual sales assistants and how much they sell to customers, it can spoil many of your efforts to make sure that customer is genuinely happy. It is impossible to create a customer-focused business while also encouraging high-pressure sales techniques.

John Lewis is well known for its profit-sharing scheme. The retailer's annual bonus scheme is based on the teams' overall performances, not on the actions of individual members. The idea behind it is that customers can rely on completely transparent advice from each salesperson, which is geared entirely to their needs, rather than the need to make a quick sale with the maximum possible profit to earn an individual a sales bonus. Meanwhile, each Partner (as John Lewis calls its employees) is incentivised to do their best within these guidelines because the company does better if they look after their customer by giving them what they really need. Their success in doing this will contribute to the overall profit of the organisation and their eventual bonus.

Many other retailers are beginning to follow this model, which is great news in my view. Carphone Warehouse, for example, does the same, and none of the team are incentivised to sell any particular phone. Bonuses are based on profits at the year end. I remember talking to Carphone Warehouse founder Charles Dunstone about the strategy. He told me he felt it was most important that no person on the team should feel pressurised to sell something to a customer that wasn't right for that customer. By making no difference to the team what they got paid on any sale, each customer could be assured they were getting the best deal that completely matched their needs.

Sandwich and coffee chain Pret A Manger has an interesting take on the idea. Pret prides itself on the personality and warmth of its staff. Each week, a mystery shopper visits every shop, looking for signs of excellent customer engagement. If the mystery shopper has a good experience, every member of the team in that branch gets an extra £1 per hour in their pay packet for the hours they worked in that week. Not surprisingly, this encourages great engagement with individual customers and 80 per cent of branches get that bonus every week.

A great part of the humanising process is for a customer to believe that the sales team in-store genuinely has their best interests at heart. The most expensive thing in the shop might be the right thing for them, but equally well, the least expensive thing might be what they want and need. It is important they are led to the right choice and know that they will be well looked after. Yes, maximising sales and profitability is a real priority of any business, but if you do it at the expense of an authentic customer relationship that business will lose out in the long run because it will leave a customer with a long-term bad feeling. Creating an environment where everybody on the sales team is rewarded for collective success will go a long way to assuaging any customer fears. Impartial advice and transparency in terms of the offer and what's best for the individual customer are critical in ultimately delivering a happy customer experience.

HUMAN INTERACTION – WINNER

Apple

It's easy to assume the secret to any Apple Store's success is its amazing tech, but it is much more than that. The philosophy of listening to the customer is built into the Apple name. Literally. The acronym APPLE spells out the exact steps of service every customer should expect.

A: Approach customers with a personalised, warm welcome.

P: Probe politely to understand the customer's needs.

P: Present a solution for the customer to take home today.

L: Listen for and resolve issues or concerns.

E: End with a fond farewell and an invitation to return.

The products in Apple's distinctive retail emporiums may change from year to year, but the five steps do not. The secret to selling products in the quantities they do, to an audience of customers who are positively evangelical about the brand, is building relationships.

The people who staff Apple Stores are chosen for the fact they are equally evangelical about the brand. They must be too, since the chain has one of the lowest turnover rates in the industry.

Apple customers are not seen as 'consumers'. They are people, and as such, want to buy from someone who sees them as individuals and who takes the time to understand their needs and modify their responses according to their specific needs. To make this happen, Apple invests a great deal in training and motivating its team. When someone walks into their store they are guaranteed to be dealing with an adviser who is not just extremely competent, but also genuinely passionate about helping them.

The experience can start outside Apple Stores before the doors are even open. If a queue has built up outside before the store opens, an Apple employee will come and talk to the people waiting and find out the reason for each individual's visit. They'll be carrying an iPad, on which they will add customers' names to waiting lists to see trouble-shooters inside the store. The store staff will be careful to explain the next steps. Once inside, a customer will be directed towards the person who can help them with their specific issue, and if it looks like there will be a wait, they'll be politely asked to browse the store for the time being, and a text will be sent the second the adviser is free. When the time comes for the appointment, the customer will inevitably be bowled over by the Apple expert's knowledge and expertise and the calm way in which problems are solved. Provided Apple continues to recruit sufficient people to match demand, it's the perfect interaction.

Language is hugely important in building the relationship. Customers are helped at 'genius bars', assistants are 'experts', and the focus of every conversation is never to 'sell' something. In fact, employees are coached in building relationships, rather than aiming to do everything they can to move the highest volume of products. Although, interestingly, by doing so, they do move a tremendous volume of products.

Apple employees are also well versed in how to handle 'difficult' customers. The key word is empathy. If someone arrives who is fed up about a smashed screen or disappointed that the gadgets are too expensive, or has lost a load of data through a system crash, Apple people employ the three 'F's: feel, felt and found. Thus, if there is a concern over price, say, they might say: 'I can see how you *feel* this way. I *felt* the price was a little high, but I *found* it is of real value because of all the built-in software and capabilities.' This empathetic response creates a connection with the customer and makes them question their original assumption. The Apple Store guy, who knows his product, thought it was worth it, so maybe they were too hasty, right?

It doesn't just end when a payment goes through the assistant's iPad and the customer is emailed a receipt. Apple wants to know what each one thinks of the experience. The organisation asks for feedback on every transaction because it wants to gauge how customers perceive them and what they can do better.

With this high level of interaction, it is no surprise that Apple has been one of the fastest growing retailers in history with an extraordinarily high rate of sales per square metre of store.

Human Interaction – Loser

Toys R Us

Anyone who has ever spent any time with young children will know that to get down to their level you need to, well, get down to their level. In other words, kneel down, squat or sit on the floor and engage. Really engage. The failure of Toys R Us in 2018 was down to many factors, but one of the prime ones was a complete lack of interaction with their customer base. There was no magic in what should have been one of the most out-of-this-world experiences for a youngster.

Toys R Us out-of-town warehouse stores with row upon row of high aisles were depressingly unimaginative. There seemed to be a mistaken belief that the toys would do the talking and create all the excitement, but of course, they didn't.

The chain failed to keep pace with, or even acknowledge, changing trends in their customers' behaviour. Children today have a very different idea of what makes a cool toy from previous generations. They are far more likely to favour anything digital, rather than traditional toys. This is no big shock though: every generation thinks the previous one is uncool and out of touch.

It would be easy to say the tendency towards digital favoured online retailers like Amazon and Game – which also has a high street presence – and that is true. But while the shift undoubtedly contributed to Toys R Us's woes, there are other toy shops on the high street that are flourishing. The Entertainer, for example, posted a 37 per cent rise in pre-tax profits a month after Toys R Us announced it was shutting all one hundred of its UK stores (Toys R Us filed for bankruptcy in the US in September 2017).

And the key to The Entertainer's success? Entertainment. The Entertainer's strategy centres on being customer focused, and staff are encouraged to deliver a stress-free shopping experience for parents, and a memorable and exciting one for kids. The emphasis of all its stores is on retail theatre, and there are lots of play spaces, shelving arranged at the right height for small people, and the tills have step stools so kids can climb up and pay for their toys themselves. Sales assistants actively demonstrate products in display areas and encourage kids to join in with great ideas such as a 'do not press' button, which when (inevitably) pressed emits ten different farting noises. Kids love it.

Toys R Us, on the other hand, never seemed to make any concerted effort to bring any sort of experimental activities into stores. When Charles Lazaras created the brand in 1957, the idea was for a 'toy supermarket' where shoppers could fill their trolleys from a vast choice of products. It was a novel idea then and it helped Toy's R Us become an industry giant. Sadly, though, the stores didn't feel much different half a century later. It appeared to trade on the fact it had long been the centre of the universe for the toy industry, even though this was far from the case for some time. Staff manned the tills and filled the shelves, but that was about as far as the interaction went.

Yes, Toys R Us faced many threats from all fronts. In addition to huge debts, Toys R Us also had to grapple with a portfolio of cavernous, uninviting warehouses at a time when the trend was towards smaller shops supported by an online offering. However, there were things it could have done. In-store, for example, it could have broken the spaces up into zones. Each zone could have represented a different experience, with staff dedicated to creating that magical moment for each child. There is still a place for 'analogue' toys, particularly in the younger market. However, loading the shelves with goods and hoping they'll sell is not good enough.

Faced with increased competition from online players, as well as big box stores like Tesco and Asda that diversified into selling toys, Toys R Us adopted a strategy of offering lower prices and a wider assortment than its competitors. It was a strategy that was never going to work. There needs to be another differentiator, and excellent customer service is the way to win. Indeed, in the toy market, perhaps more so than in any other, attentive, innovative and entertaining customer service has to be a priority. There has to be a compelling reason for customers to visit.

Step Five

Make Mistakes . . . Lots

Key Points

- The customer is always right may be an old adage, but fewer and fewer businesses seem to respect it. Always put things right. Fast.
- When something goes wrong, let the person who receives the complaint 'own' it and see it through to resolution. Directing an already fed up customer through to a lengthy, disconnected, bureaucratic process is a recipe for disaster.

One of the oldest adages of all about customer service must surely be: the customer is always right. There is a legendary customer service story about Nordstrom to which you could add, even when they are probably wrong. It remains one of the greatest examples of exemplary customer relations of all times. Nordstrom, which began life as a shoe store in Seattle in 1901, grew to become one of America's most renowned fashion speciality chains on the back of the excellent way it treated all customers. The chain's success was predicated on its absolute no-quibble returns policy. This strategy was pursued to such an extent that a customer services clerk did not bat an eyelid when a man walked into a Nordstrom store in Fairbanks, Alaska, carrying two tyres and asked for his money back. The clerk simply checked the price on the side of the tyres, opened the cash register and handed the sum over. Not once did the Nordstrom employee mention that the upmarket store only ever sold clothing and had never, ever, diversified into automotive parts.

It's an extreme example, but listening to, and putting right, customer concerns is a key part of helping them to feel happy about shopping with you. The customer *is* always right if you wish to see them return to you.

Just as in the Nordstrom story, they may not be 100 per cent right in the true sense of the word. However, what is crucial here is how a store deals with their complaint. Get it wrong, or deal with their complaints in an uninterested or patronising manner, and all that hard work to ease their journey, read their mood and give great service will be wasted. Not only will you have lost a loyal customer, but the backlash can have devastating consequences too. In the digital age, literally thousands of people will get to hear about it if a retailer's service does not come up to scratch and they show no interest in rectifying the situation. The old maxim that an unhappy customer will tell a dozen or so of their friends is just a distant memory. Today, the potential is seemingly endless and the worse the screw-up, the more widely the story is likely to spread. And customers take a lot of notice of disgruntled reviews, blogs and tweets. More than one third of those with access to the internet in the UK say they have chosen not to buy a product as a result of online comments from customers or other private individuals.[3] Online giants like Amazon and eBay have even pushed this dynamic one stage further by actively encouraging customers to post feedback on both the product and the service provided. If you are not looking after your customers properly and/ or dealing with their complaints adequately, there really is nowhere to hide.

[3] Ipsos MORI Technology Tracker.

Despite all of this, no business should fear complaints. In fact, I would urge any retailer to view it as a massive opportunity. Knowing what you are *not doing well* is just as, if not more, important than knowing what makes your clientele happy. Not only can you fix whatever isn't happening to a satisfactory standard, thus ensuring a loyal and happy customer, but you can also open up the possibility of them spending more money each time they visit. Why? Because now they will fully trust you and will relax in the knowledge you are fully able to own any mistakes and put them right as soon as they are raised.

Ask anyone to tell you a great customer service story about John Lewis or Waitrose and I wager that nine out of ten will tell you about something that went wrong but was brilliantly put right. Perhaps the wrong TV was delivered or the washing machine was scratched, but each time, after a phone call and a quick explanation, a colleague would leap into action and make sure the problem was remedied. The Partnership even has a dedicated budget for what it calls 'Goodwill'. In the past as much as 2 per cent of the sales budget was spent on putting things right for customers when they'd gone wrong.

At Waitrose there is a no-quibble policy on refunds. If a customer wasn't happy, we'd refund and replace. At a minimum, a customer would get a replacement product, or an alternative, *and* we'd give them another one to try free of charge. We made a great deal out of it too. Colleagues were encouraged to thank customers for coming back and saying; this wasn't very good. With that feedback we were able to make the business stronger.

I recall an interesting debate I had with Tim Steiner when he was first setting up Ocado, the home delivery service. He told me that his goal was to build processes that mitigated every customer error because he wanted to have minimal customer complaints. He said that if Ocado didn't have a particular product line available, it was automatically taken off the website until it was back in stock. This way, customers would not ever be disappointed by a notice saying: 'I'm sorry, your favourite brand X baked beans aren't available.' Instead, all the alternative brands were listed, with no mention of brand X.

I questioned the philosophy at the time, telling Tim I loved customer complaints. The reason I really liked them was because if you do things really well to resolve problems for a customer, they become a huge fan. What's more they would tell everyone they knew how well their problem was sorted out.

If I had been in Tim's position, I would have listed brand X, and if a customer was unhappy about the lack of availability I would say that next time they ordered they could have their regular can for free. The cost would have been minimal, maybe a couple of pounds. That's nothing, particularly in relations to the thousands of pounds many organisations spend on their marketing, but imagine how powerful that would be for a customer? Complaints and putting things right are always, always an opportunity.

Personalise Complaints

What better way could there be to show that you love and value a customer than by instantly putting something right after it has gone wrong? Yet, I'm frequently amazed that this is not the norm everywhere I go. All too often, people bring a problem to a business's attention and the spotlight is immediately turned on the complainant.

'Really? Are you sure about that?'

'Do you have a receipt?'

'Are you sure you set it up properly?'

Worse still, some businesses seek to de-humanise the process completely, pushing it as far away as they possibly can. The person that receives the complaint says it is not something they can possibly deal with in-store and the customer will have to ring a call centre. A call centre! Now, I am all for businesses driving efficiencies, but I have to say that moving complaints handling to an anonymous call centre is about the worst possible example of customer service. This means driving customers out of the store and onto the phone with someone they don't know, can't see and who probably has marginal interest in or insight into the issue. It's enough to drive a person mad. The complaint and, more importantly, the complainant becomes completely disconnected from the original store. More often than not, the customer is then led into a spiral of frustration that will almost certainly end with a vow to never, ever shop with that particular store ever again.

In the last section, we talked about the importance of the human touch and this is even more important when something goes wrong. As everyone knows, in a situation like this, all you want is for someone to listen, empathise and promise to do all they can to put things right. Better still, that they themselves will deal with the problem and follow it through until a satisfactory solution is found. Directing someone to a call centre doesn't come close to dealing with the issue.

Why do stores do this? They are not only absolving themselves from the complainant, they are absolving themselves from any valuable learning experience too. By not hearing a customer's view first-hand, they lose a priceless source of information about underlying problems with their products and services, which could very well prevent further issues coming up. I am at a loss to understand why any business spends a fortune on satisfaction surveys and performance benchmarking exercises, while chasing any dissatisfied customers off the premises. They are the very people who can give an honest appraisal about the service being received. They have sound evidence on how things could instantly be improved.

Shops that do deal with complaints on the ground may also be tempted to introduce procedures to record and track complaints. This is commendable, and a perfect learning situation. However, once again, it shouldn't happen at the expense of personally dealing with the problem as swiftly as humanly possible. If there is technology involved to log complaints, keep things as simple and relevant as possible. This is not a market research exercise where a store seeks to capture as much information as possible about a customer's shopping habits. The onus is always on *solving* the problem and learning from it. Expecting a customer to fill out a lengthy questionnaire with no real sign of progress is only going to antagonise them further.

When I ran Waitrose I was so convinced of this course of action I moved customer complaint handling, as far as possible, back to the shops. If a customer emailed or called head office their concern was put back to the local branch to deal with. They had the authority to put things right for the customer. Only direct sales complaints or litigation were handled via a central team. Not only did it give customers a more immediate route to resolve their issues, it also saved time and cost. The longer a complaint goes on, the more expensive it tends to be to resolve. And in all likelihood the call centre will contact the branch for information. That means the cost of handling is also increased with the service centre acting as an intermediary. With higher costs, a less good service and a shop team absolved of responsibility for putting right the thing that has gone wrong, I am challenged to see the benefits of centralising the service.

Make Mistakes – Winner

Co-op

The Co-op has had its fair share of challenges in recent years. Discounters, such as Aldi and Lidl, took a chunk of its core market and online grocers have been making slow, but steady inroads into it as well. Then a crisis at the Co-operative Bank marred the group and the bank needed to be saved from collapse in 2013. (It has since sold its stake in the lender.) A series of leaks about management and boardroom spats just added to the feeling that the retailer was in big trouble.

Although Co-op has been ruthless in restructuring and refocusing the group in past years, selling off many non-core businesses and partnering with Costcutter to become its exclusive wholesale supplier, it recognised that recent events had been very damaging indeed. Its 54,000 employees were shaken by the uncertainty over their futures, even though things were apparently being turned around, and its millions of members also felt unsettled. Even day-to-day customers saw enough media coverage to wonder what was going on.

Although the pressure from rival retailers is not going to go away, Co-op is putting its faith in its team to spread its message as it strives to rebuild itself for a stronger future. Beginning with a survey to find out how its employees felt about the retailer, it discovered that there was still a great deal of loyalty to the brand and that the team craved a more meaningful relationship with it. Despite its problems, colleagues still wanted to shout about the Co-op, an organisation that continues to stir a great deal of pride within them thanks to the way it has long championed community, social and sustainability goals.

A campaign called #beingcoop was designed to empower colleagues and revitalise the brand. The idea behind it was to create a workplace that celebrates difference, where employees could feel responsible, valued and trusted to do the right thing for each other, members and customers. The four values that encapsulated #beingcoop were: do what matters most; be yourself always; show you care; and succeed together.

The #beingcoop message was communicated to staff via face-to-face sessions across the country. The sessions mixed people from different departments to encourage integration. People from individual stores were encouraged to get involved in the local communities they served. One store in Nottingham, for example, developed a close working relationship with a specialist school for children with Asperger's syndrome, raising awareness and taking children on work placements. In another store, the manager learned sign language in order to be better able to communicate with deaf customers.

Everyday thank-you kits were introduced to recognise colleagues for #beingcoop in the moment. Store managers are empowered to reward colleagues for bringing the Co-op values to life and have a range of gifts to choose from within the pack, with thank you cards, gift bags, wine bags and a very popular 'Thank you for Being Co-op' selfie frame. Everyone is encouraged to share their stories of the great things their colleagues are doing to help their customers and local communities for a #beingcoop wall of fame. In 2018, Co-op held its first ever 'Thank you for Being Co-op' awards, celebrating colleagues who went the extra mile to help customers and make their mark on the local community.

Of course, establishing trust between a brand and its customers is not something that happens overnight. Not everything can go right in any retail operation, and therefore the way Co-op handled complaints was paramount to its revival. The Co-op customer relations operation, which is made up of 25 staff, handles up to 60,000 complaints and queries each year. The contact centre was put at the heart of the plan to reboot the company. Previous refund limits were removed and advisers were given discretion to purchase personal gifts from a dedicated Amazon account in order to compensate disgruntled customers. Targets were set on the time it took to resolve a complaint, bringing it down from an average of seven days to two. The team is now developing a pre-emptive strategy to spot and satisfy a potentially unhappy customer before they even complain!

Competition is still tough on the high street, but Co-op is undoubtedly distinguishing itself, and employee engagement and customer services are at the heart of that.

MAKE MISTAKES – LOSER

Best Buy

Customer service is all about expectations. When someone walks into a store, they have made a choice to do so. Very often, this choice is made based on past experiences or from experiences with a similar business. It's an unspoken trust, but a powerful one. Thus, if a retailer makes a customer a promise, the customer believes what they are told. And why not?

The penalties for getting this wrong are high. US electronics dealer, Best Buy, managed to upset legions of customers with one of its marketing efforts. Then, to compound the misery, stayed stoically quiet in the aftermath, which ensured a whole lot more people got to hear about it as enraged customers vented their anger on social media.

A few years back, Best Buy decided to boost sales with some incredible Black Friday-style discounts. They were promoted aggressively online too. Naturally, its customers were delighted to get their Christmas shopping done early and on a budget. They paid for their goods and sat back to wait for them to be delivered, content that they had done a major part of their festive shopping.

Then, just days before Christmas, Best Buy got in touch with its customers to say they were out of stock.

'Overwhelming demand of hot product offerings,' was cited as the reason why Best Buy would not be able to deliver the goods before Christmas. 'We have encountered a situation that has affected redemption of some of our customers' online orders.'

Not surprisingly, customers were enraged. The community forums on Best Buy's website were filled with furious complaints. One thread was called: 'I would like to thank Best Buy for killing Christmas'. Another simply referred to the retailer as the 'Grinch'. Words like 'thieves', 'boycott' and 'scam' were freely used and some unhappy customers helpfully listed alternative places people might like to shop in the future. It wasn't just confined to the Best Buy site either. Furious shoppers lit up the web with angry comments.

Most infuriatingly, Best Buy, which once prided

itself on its use of social media to engage customers, was surprisingly low key in its response. A statement of apology was issued to select media outlets, but for a while it failed to even acknowledge the problem on its Twitter feed or Facebook page. When it did eventually admit an unacceptable delay between order confirmations and notices of cancellations, it wasn't enough to calm down the backlash. Best Buy had not delivered (in all senses of the word) and it had not met customer expectations.

To compound the problem, some in-store staff told fed up customers that they were being prevented by head office from offering similarly priced, alternative models. Customers reported being offered older models of the product they wanted to buy, but at a higher price. It appeared that no concessions whatsoever were made to customers to make up for the catastrophic error.

It would be too simplistic to equate this disaster with Best Buy's falling profits and multiple store closures that happened in the immediate aftermath, but there is no doubt that it had an impact. In this case, Best Buy did the very opposite of the maxim: under promise and over deliver.

Step Six

Empower Your Team

Key Point

- If you empower the team, giving them freedom, trust and autonomy, they will reward you by becoming more productive. Most importantly, they will be fixated on pleasing the customer.

Whenever a new director started at Waitrose I would remind them that while their job carried with it a huge amount of responsibility, there were others in our organisation who played a far more impactful role.

'You're going to make really big strategic decisions that are going to impact the lives of 60,000 people,' I'd say. 'But never forget that there's a cashier in the King's Road branch that looks after 200 customers a day. It is in their power to make a customer feel great about shopping with us, or not. So what are you doing to help that person feel empowered?'

In my view, the most crucial role my senior staff could play was in maximising the happiness of the team around them. Happy employees give more, which means customers get more.

The empowerment of a team has been at the heart of the John Lewis Partnership's success ever since its founder, John Spedan Lewis, declared that if all employees were given a share in profits, as well as information on how the company is doing and the power to influence its direction, it would be better for everyone. Even though I have now left the organisation, I still passionately believe in the power of making employees a key part of the decision-making process, listening to their ideas and integrating their suggestions into a business's strategy.

The supreme purpose of the John Lewis Partnership is the happiness of its employees. The organisation's founder believed that if you didn't have happy employees you couldn't hope to have happy customers.

Reward your team by giving them freedom, power, trust, autonomy and encouragement, and they will be more productive because they feel more in control. Allowing employees to make decisions on their own and letting them experience the success that follows, helps them feel valued and rewarded. They associate success with their own abilities, which in turn motivates them to strive for more in future tasks. This makes people more willing to work together, manage tasks and suggest better ways of doing things. Most importantly, in this context, it ensures they are 100 per cent focused on pleasing the customer. Only they can deliver a great and happy experience, and the only way to ensure this is if they're engaged and happy too.

Empowerment of a team is not just paying lip service to inclusiveness while at the same time expecting people to work 12 hour days on zero-hour contracts. If a company doesn't show it is genuinely invested in its team, they will inevitably feel like cannon fodder. When a customer complains, they won't rush to solve the issue. Why would they? It's not worth the aggravation if you are not emotionally invested in the business.

We had a huge number of ways to empower the team at the Partnership, which are fully documented in my book *Fairness for All*. Partners are invited to vote on key decisions and elect representatives to both the

Partnership Council and the Board. The use of the vote in the Partnership is a mechanism for ensuring that management is accountable to the workforce. Managers are free to manage, but at the same time need to do so according to the interests of the co-owners and with full accountability to the managed. To actively encourage a two-way dialogue there is a wide-range of initiatives in place so every Partner has a say in the way the business is run, right down to the fact every single Partner is free to walk up and ask any director or senior manager a direct question about the business or make a suggestion. This is not a chore for management. In fact, it is a source of invaluable insight. The notion that workers can't possibly have anything of use to contribute belongs firmly in the last century.

Everything is devolved, right down to the opening hours of individual stores. Branches can decide what is right for their particular area, depending on the local clientele. Indeed, Partners are regularly asked to come up with suggestions on everything from improving the working day, to big ideas on the future direction of the company.

In the previous section we looked at the benefits of handling customer complaints effectively. Empowering the team is central to this strategy. In the Partnership, authority to deal with complaints has been devolved to the lowest level. Partners know that if someone comes in and something is not right, it is in their gift to put it right. How they choose to resolve the issue is up to them.

Many organisations are very prescriptive about the way complaints are dealt with. Some even paste a set of rather forbidding rules on the wall behind the cash tills headed by the statement 'No refunds!'. This attitude completely ignores the fact that the person on the ground is the one facing the shopper, who may be furious about something that seems to have gone wrong. They are without a doubt in the best position to decide upon the best course of action. It is their business and these are their customers. If they want to see them again, they'll make the right call. They are trusted to make sensible decisions and they invariably do.

Devolving power like this will feel quite strange to many organisations. It may feel counter-intuitive to focus the bulk of its attention inwardly, particularly if there is an acceptance that, yes, the customer is the number one priority. However, if employees don't feel engaged in the company, they won't invest their time and passion into its success. This means the service they deliver will inevitably be below par, and customers will notice that and will suffer because of it. Ironically, since this is the final section of the six, empowering the team is actually the starting point of delivering a great service.

EMPOWER YOUR TEAM – WINNER

Argos

Argos has an affectionate nickname for the 30,000 employees who work on the front line in its 755 stores or at its distribution centres. They're known as the firm's 'digital army'. The high street chain recognises that without their passionate input, it won't stand a chance in its desire to become a leading digital retailer.

With a declared strategy of 'customers first, colleagues always', Argos's digital army have been at the hub of an interesting and successful transformation. Early on in the 2000s, Argos was in real danger of slipping behind because its model of ordering by catalogue and collecting in-store looked a little tired and old-fashioned compared to newer, more technologically developed rivals. In late 2012, the store announced ambitious plans to reinvent itself as a digital retail leader.

There were three key elements to the strategy. The first was to always, always, fulfil all promises made online. If a customer found and then reserved a product on their iPad and then discovered it was out of stock when the system had said otherwise, that was a lost customer. Secondly, that the website must work seamlessly on mobile devices. Thirdly, and most importantly, to encourage and enable the team so they are able to deliver on the promise of 'more choice, available faster'. Argos is working on a strategy so that customers who have ordered and paid can come in-store, collect the product, and leave again within 60 seconds if they wish. The only way the retailer can achieve this is through total commitment from the team. They need to work together to move stock around easily and get it to customers quickly.

Digital retailers always make much of the value of the 'seamless' customer experience, where customers move from viewing a product on an app on their phone to taking it home. Providing a seamless experience might look, well, seamless, but it actually requires a lot of coordination. In the background there is a large team of people synchronising information such as prices, special offers and stock availability, coordinating with web designers and distributors and, of course, in Argos's case, there is the person on the front line who is dealing with the customer in-store.

When Argos was first planning the strategy to become a leading digital retailer, the senior team realised its success relied on the way they dealt with customers in-store. This meant there needed to be a number of strategic changes to the way its colleagues operated. Traditionally, Argos stores were large open spaces, with rows of tables for catalogues, a collection counter and some tills. If a customer wanted to speak with a member of staff, they'd need to approach them at the collection counter or till. While they no doubt got a friendly reception, the onus was on the customer to do the walking and talking. It should, of course, be the other way around. Argos invested in training to get colleagues to engage with customers, and employees were brought out from behind the counters and the tills and moved to a better location in the centre of the store. Colleagues were schooled in how to interact with customers and also on how to spot someone who looked in need of some help.

The philosophy of the company is to be constantly inclusive, and it therefore runs surveys on a number of topics, from changes in uniform to comments on the new strategy. One-off campaigns such as 'Be the Big Difference' drive the inclusiveness message home by showing colleagues that the smallest contribution can make the biggest difference to customers and colleagues.

The 'customers first, colleagues always' strategy has had a huge impact on the retailer's vision for a digitally led future and has firmly reversed declines in performance and profitability, leading to their purchase by Sainsbury's.

EMPOWER YOUR TEAM – LOSER

Store Twenty One

It's a familiar story: when sales begin to fall, staff numbers usually rapidly follow the same pattern. The correlation most probably makes perfect sense to management, who view the spreadsheet and place great importance on the balance between sales targets and the payroll. Ergo: when sales dip, payroll does too. The thinking may go that customers may not even notice a few less people about the place. Certainly, less so than reduced stock on the rails or threadbare carpets.

This is a completely misguided strategy and can have a hugely damaging effect that can quickly put a store into a downward spiral.

Read about any retail failure – and there are depressingly many to choose from today – and you'll usually see that staff numbers have been cut in the run up to the final death knell. Often dramatically so. Budget fashion and homewares retail chain Store Twenty One went into administration in the summer of 2017. Store Twenty One started life in the 1930s as a manufacturing business, supplying retailers such as Marks & Spencer. It went on to open its own branches, which sold seconds, before changing tack once more when it was rebranded as QS in the 1980s and then as Store Twenty One in the early 2000s after being acquired by Indian textile company Alok Group. After struggling for a long while, the 122-store chain closed its doors and 900 staff lost their jobs. However, by this time, staff numbers were well down from previous levels. The store's difficulties were blamed on the current economy and tough times on the high street, but while this was undoubtedly a factor, it could also be argued that failing to work with, and empower the team could have contributed too. There were also reports that some staff didn't get paid in the months leading up to the chain's demise.

Staff levels are crucial and have an impact in so many different ways. The most obvious is that there are always enough people around the place to assist customers should they need it. There is nothing worse than a fruitless in-store hunt for someone, anyone, to help with a query. They also play an important role in keeping the store well stocked and presentable. People on the shop floor are always the first to spot poorly selling or obsolete goods that should be returned to the distribution centre rather than taking up valuable shelf space that could be filled with better performing items. Plus, since they are on the front line and interacting with customers, they are in pole position to spot evolving new trends. Instead of taking a pen to staff numbers, store management should be finding ways to engage with their colleagues so they can find out what will sell like hot cakes. Engaged staff will put any store ahead of the curve.

While cost reductions can be essential for a retailer's survival when times are tough, it can be argued that cutting staff numbers should be the last resort. A good number of engaged colleagues is critical. Reducing numbers inevitably reduces customer service and erodes a retailer's brand. If cuts are required, whatever cost-cutting initiatives are chosen, I would be hugely wary of anything that delivers a reduced or inferior service or a reduction in the overall quality of the experience. It is a slippery slope.

Conclusion

If I were to take four key lessons from my three decades in retailing they would be these.

Love the customers you have. Increasing your retention rate by just 5 per cent will add 25–95 per cent to your profits. A far bigger impact than adding 5 per cent new customers.

Value, train and retain the employees you have. It's your employees who deliver to your customers. If you put them and their happiness first, they can be truly engaged in their jobs and in your organisation's success. Your staff turnover will be lower, your sick absence lower, your productivity and profits higher.

Retailing is a team sport. It's unlikely that one genius at the top will make a sustained difference. One hundred times 1 per cent improvements are easier to achieve than 1 times 100 per cent improvement. Ask your whole team how you keep finding those continuous improvements.

Take the time to understand what 'great service' looks like so you can explain it in detail.

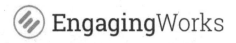 **Engaging**Works

Helping you have a happier working life at
www.engaging.works

• Find work

Develop your career, communicate and connect and build
a business library – all in one place.

• Global Hub

The global hub brings the world of business to you. You
can post content, ask for expert advice, watch and listen
to lectures and tutorials, read articles, find out about
forthcoming events and view job vacancies.

• Messenger

Securely communicate with your business network.
Build your network and form project groups. (Also
available on iOS and Android)

• Video and conference calling

Available as part of our premium service you can make
unlimited calls with unlimited participants.

• Mentoring

Register to be a mentor or mentee and connect via our
messenger service.

ALSO AVAILABLE FROM MARK PRICE: